Lecture Notes in Computer Science 3161

Commenced Publication in 1973
Founding and Former Series Editors:
Gerhard Goos, Juris Hartmanis, and Jan van Leeuwen

Massimo Tistarelli   Josef Bigun
Enrico Grosso

Advanced Studies in Biometrics

Summer School on Biometrics
Alghero, Italy, June 2-6, 2003
Revised Selected Lectures and Papers

 Springer

Authors

Massimo Tistarelli
Enrico Grosso
University of Sassari, Computer Vision Laboratory
Palazzo del Pou Salit - Piazza Duomo 6, 07041 Alghero (SS), Italy
E-mail: {tista,grosso}@uniss.it

Josef Bigun
University of Halmstad, IDE
Box 823, 301 18 Halmstad, Sweden
E-mail: Josef.Bigun@ide.hh.se

Library of Congress Control Number: 2005926703

CR Subject Classification (1998): I.5, I.4, I.3, K.6.5

ISSN   0302-9743
ISBN-10   3-540-26204-0 Springer Berlin Heidelberg New York
ISBN-13   978-3-540-26204-6 Springer Berlin Heidelberg New York

Springer is a part of Springer Science+Business Media

springeronline.com

© Springer-Verlag Berlin Heidelberg 2005
Printed in Germany

Typesetting: Camera-ready by author, data conversion by Boller Mediendesign
Printed on acid-free paper   SPIN: 11493648   06/3142   5 4 3 2 1 0

Preface to the Lectures Book of the 1st Summer School for Advanced Studies on Biometrics 2003

Springer LNCS 3161

The ability to automatically recognize an individual has increasingly been acknowledged as a significant step in many application domains. In the last decade, several recognition and identification systems based on biometric measurements have been proposed. Many different biological signals have been utilized: fingerprints, face and facial features, retinal scans, iris patterns, hand geometry, DNA traces, and gait, and others. Not only have research tools been developed, but a notable number of new applications have been observed, making studies on biometrics a very stimulating but also a challenging arena.

All these issues pushed us to organize the 1st Summer School on Biometrics, which addressed the two facets of personal identity authentication: verification and identification. The school not only stressed the different techniques involved in the two processes, but also provided an in-depth roadmap on the algorithmic and technological issues involved in the development and integration of biometric systems.

This special LNCS volume offers the efforts and major achievements of both the school lecturers and some of the most outstanding students in the classes. The papers present different biometric authentication techniques in an attempt to provide a comprehensive selection of state-of-the-art methods used to address applications demanding robust solutions.

The volume is divided into two parts. The first part, composed of seven papers, covers a selection of the lectures given at the school classes, while the second part contains the four best contributions of the students.

In Part I, the first paper, by Bigun et al., covers a topic expected to alleviate concerns on performance and convenience, a combination of several sensing modalities or multimodal biometrics. The lecture discusses major issues involved in multi-biometrics to improve machine recognition performance while it exposes some recent findings on the human ability in person recognition. The second and third papers, by Boyd and Little, and Maltoni, respectively, address two specific biometric modalities: gait and fingerprint recognition. These papers describe two classical examples of behavioral (gait recognition) and physiological (fingerprint recognition) biometric modalities. The paper by Boyd and Little presents the psychophysics of gait recognition and different computational models to process image sequences to extract dynamic information for recognition. The paper by Maltoni is a comprehensive tutorial on fingerprint recognition, describing in detail all relevant issues in data acquisition and processing, including the latest advances in the state of the art. The fourth paper, by Tistarelli et al., analyzes the biological motivations for face-based authentication. The lecture, while exploring the psychophysics of human vision relevant to person authentication, highlights several biologically inspired processes to improve automatic face-based recognition. The application of statistical classifiers and the learning theory for robust biometric authentication are discussed in the fifth paper, by Verri et al. The application of support vector machines, firstly proposed by V. Vapnik, to biometric authentication and recognition is fully described. The sixth paper, by Yeshurun and Dganit, describes an exciting methodology and practice when using hand recognition. This contribution is well coupled with the last paper in this part, by Cipolla et al., which describes an interesting methodology to detect and track human gestures. A remarkable difference from other approaches is the use of 3D rather than 2D information for hand tracking and gesture recognition.

The presentations from the students, which we found to deserve further attention from the scientific community, were chosen to be included In Part II. The first student paper, by Castellani et al., introduces an interesting technique to exploit 3D stereoscopic data for face recognition. On a similar topic is the last paper in this section, by Conde et al.; in this case the influence of feature localization accuracy for classification is addressed. The second paper, by Gokberk et al., applies genetic algorithms to drive the feature extraction process. The proposed model is applied to a set of facial features extracted from Gabor filtered images. The paper by Campadelli and Lanzarotti, the third in this part, describes a novel method for face recognition based on elastic bunch graph matching. Differently from other approaches the set of features (jets vector) is extracted automatically from gray level and color images.

Last but not least, we wish to thank all lecturers and students and others who actively cooperated to make this event. We hope that the school contributed to the dissemination of state of the art in biometrics, as well as to advanced studies of it.

Massimo Tistarelli
Josef Bigun
Enrico Grosso

Table of Contents

Combining Biometric Evidence for Person Authentication   1
J. Bigun, J. Fierrez-Aguilar, J. Ortega-Garcia, J. Gonzales-Rodriguez

Biometric Gait Recognition 19
J.E. Boyd, J.J. Little

A Tutorial on Fingerprint Recognition 43
D. Maltoni

Spiral Topologies for Biometric Recognition 69
M. Tistarelli, E. Grosso, A. Lagorio

Statistical Learning Approaches with Application to Face Detection 91
E. Franceschi, F. Odone, A. Verri

Hand Detection by Direct Convexity Estimation 105
D. Maimon, Y. Yeshurun

Template-Based Hand Detection and Tracking 114
R. Cipolla, B. Stenger, A. Thayananthan, P.H.S. Torr

Student Papers

3D Face Recognition Using Stereoscopic Vision 126
U. Castellani, M. Bicego, G. Iacono, V. Murino

Selection of Location, Frequency, and Orientation Parameters of
2D Gabor Wavelets for Face Recognition 138
B. Gökberk, M.O. Irfanoglu, L. Akarun, E. Alpaydın

A Face Recognition System Based on Local Feature Characterization 147
P. Campadelli, R. Lanzarotti

Influence of Location over Several Classifiers in 2D and 3D Face
Verification 153
S. Mata, C. Conde, A. Sánchez, E. Cabello

Author Index 159

Combining Biometric Evidence for Person Authentication

J. Bigun[1], J. Fierrez-Aguilar[2*], J. Ortega-Garcia[2], and J. Gonzalez-Rodriguez[2]

[1] Halmstad University, Sweden
josef.bigun@ide.hh.se
[2] Universidad Politecnica de Madrid, Spain
{jfierrez,jortega,jgonzalez}@diac.upm.es

Abstract. Humans are excellent experts in person recognition and yet they do not perform excessively well in recognizing others only based on one modality such as single facial image. Experimental evidence of this fact is reported concluding that even human authentication relies on multimodal signal analysis. The elements of automatic multimodal authentication along with system models are then presented. These include the machine experts as well as machine supervisors. In particular, fingerprint and speech based systems will serve as illustration. A signal adaptive supervisor based on the input biometric signal quality is evaluated. Experimental results on data collected from a mobile telephone prototype application are reported demonstrating the benefits of the reported scheme.

1 Introduction

Face recognition is an important element of person authentication in humans. Human face analysis engages special signal processing in visual cortex different than processing of other objects [2, 3]. It is reliably observed in a number of studies that negative bias in ability to recognize faces of another racial group versus own racial group exists [4, 5, 6]. It has been confirmed that the hair style and facial expressions are significant distraction factors for humans. It has recently been revealed [7] that the lack of caricature type information hampers the recognition more than the lack of silhouette and shading information and that there is a gender bias in women's and and men's abilities to recognize faces. In [7] it is shown that, depending on the gender to be recognized, humans were able to recognize unfamiliar faces from photographs at the success rate of 55-75%. This suggests that multimodal biometric information processing e.g. using signals from body motion including the head motion, speech, and lip movements, plays a significant role in human's efforts of authenticating other humans.

Automatic access of persons to services is becoming increasingly important in the information era. Although person authentication by machine has been a

---

* This study has been carried out while J. F.-A. and J. O.-G. were guest scientists at Halmstad University [1].

M. Tistarelli, J. Bigun, and E. Grosso (Eds.): Biometrics School 2003, LNCS 3161, pp. 1–18, 2005.

subject of study for more than thirty years [8, 9], it has not been until recently that the matter of combining a number of different traits for person verification has been considered [10, 11]. There are a number of benefits of doing so, just to name a few: false acceptance and false rejection error rates decrease, the authentication system becomes more robust against individual sensor or subsystem failures and the number of cases where the system is not able to give an answer (e.g. bad quality fingerprints due to manual work or larynx disorders) vanishes. The technological environment is also appropriate because of the widespread deployment of multimedia-enabled mobile devices (PDAs, 3G mobile phones, tablet PCs, laptops on wireless LANs, etc.). As a result, much research work is currently being done in order to fulfill the requirements of applications for masses.

Two early sound theoretical frameworks for combining different machine experts in a multimodal biometric system are described in [11] and [12], the former from a risk analysis perspective [13] and the later from a statistical pattern recognition point of view [14]. Both of them concluded (under some mild conditions which normally hold in practice) that the weighted average is a good way of conciliating the different experts. Soon after, multimodal fusion was studied as a two-class classification problem by using a number of machine learning paradigms [15, 16, 17], for example: neural networks, decision trees and support vector machines. They too confirmed the benefits of performance gains with trained classifiers, and favored support vector machines over neural networks and decision trees. The architecture of the system, ease of training, ease of implementation and generalization to mass use were however not considered in these studies. As happens in every pattern recognition problem which is application-oriented, these are important issues that influence the choice of a supervisor.

Interestingly enough, some recent works have nevertheless reported comparable performance between fixed and trained combining strategies [18, 19] and a debate has come out investigating the benefits of both approaches [20, 21]. As an example, and within this debate, some researches have shown how to learn user-specific parameters in a trained fusion scheme [22, 23]. As a result, they have showed that the overall verification performance can be improved significantly by considering user-dependent fusion schemes.

In this work we focus on some other benefits of a trained fusion strategy. In particular, an adaptive trained fusion scheme is introduced here. With adaptive fusion scheme, we mean that the supervisor readapts to each identity claim as a function of the quality of the input biometric signal, usually depending on external conditions such as light and background noise. Furthermore, experiments on real data from a prototype mobile authentication application combining fingerprint and speech data are reported.

This paper is structured as follows. In Section 2, we summarize the findings on mono-modal human recognition performance suggesting that individual modalities do not have to score high to yield robust multimodal systems [7]. Beginning in section 3 with some definitions, we discuss machine supervisors for multimodal authentication [1, 11] in the sequel. The elements of multimodal authentication along with major notations are introduced in section 4. In section 5, the statistical framework for conciliating the different expert opinions together with simplified and full supervisor algorithms are described. The components of our prototype mobile authentication application, namely fingerprint and speaker verification subsystems, are briefly described in section 6. Some experiments are reported in section 8 using the above mentioned multimodal authentication prototype and the performance evaluation methodology described in section 7. Conclusions will be finally given in section 9.

2   Human Face Recognition Performance

There is a general agreement on that, approximately at the age of 12 the performance of children in face recognition reaches adult levels, that there is already an impressive face recognition ability by the age of 5 and that measurable preferences for face stimuli exist in babies even younger than 10 minutes [24].

Our study [7], that aimed at quantifying the skills of humans in face recognition of unfamiliar faces, has been supported by more than 4000 volunteers[3]. We found that the lack of high spatial frequencies in visual stimuli, which result in blurred images as if face information were coming from an unfocused camera, hamper the recognition significantly more than the lack of low spatial frequencies, which result in stimuli similar to artist drawn faces, see Figure 1.

The face recognition questions. In all 8 questions (Q1-Q8) the task was to identify the picture of a stimulus person among a query set consisting of 10 pictures. The subjects were informed, before the start of the test, that the stimulus image and the image to be found in the query set were taken at two different occasions and that these two images could differ significantly in hair style, glasses, expression of the face, facial hair, clothing, etc. due to the natural changes in appearance that occur upon passage of time (a few months). In Q1-Q4 and Q8 the stimulus and the query set were shown simultaneously, in the same screen. Questions Q5-Q7 were similar to the other questions except that they included a memorization task in that the stimulus was shown in its own page without the query set. When the subject wished to continue, the stimulus was replaced by the query set, forcing the subjects to answer the question without a possibility to see the stimulus.

The available results [7] reveal that in questions in which the face image to be recognized was not manipulated (e.g. the high frequencies were not depreciated), the recognition rate varied between 55-75 % in the average. A surprising result was that the females had in the average better success in all tasks than the males. A typical question in the test is illustrated by Figure 1.

The fact that the success rates are in the best cases (female subjects) around 80% suggests that not only mono-modal information but also multimodal biometric information processing e.g. using the signals from body motion including head motion, speech, and lip movements, plays a significant role when humans authenticate other humans.

---

[3] As of November 2003. The test is available at http://www.hh.se/facetest

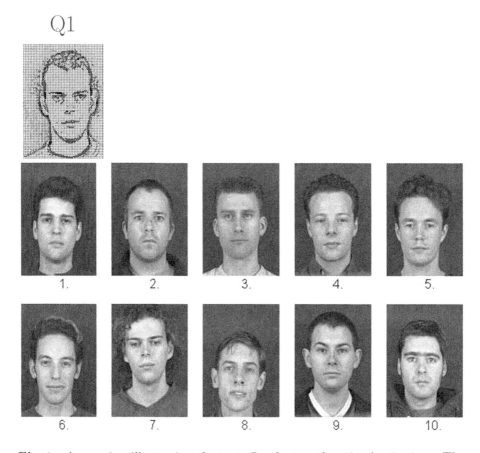

Fig. 1. A question illustrating the test. On the top the stimulus is given. The subject matched the stimulus with one of the 10 images below the stimulus. The low spatial frequencies of the stimulus were removed by signal processing.

3   Definitions

In *authentication* (also known as *verification*) applications, the users or *clients* are known to the system whereas the *impostors* can potentially be the world population. In such applications the users provide their claimed identities (either true or false) and a one-to-one matching is performed. If the result of the comparison (also *score* or *opinion*) is higher than a *verification threshold*, then the claim is accepted, otherwise the claim is rejected.

In *identification* applications, there is no identity claim and the candidate is compared to a database of client models, therefore a one-to-many matching is performed in this case. In the simplest form of identification, also known as *closed-set identification*, the best client model is selected. In *open-set identification*, the highest score is further compared to a verification threshold so as

Fig. 2. The proposed system model of multi-modal person authentication.

to accept/reject this candidate as belonging or not to the database (an implicit authentication step).

In a multimodal authentication framework, various subsystems (also denoted as *experts*) are present, each one of them specialized on a different trait. Each expert delivers its opinion on a "package" of data containing an identity claim (e.g. face images, fingerprint images, speech data, etc.) that will be referred to as a *shot*. This paper is focused on combining the experts opinions (also known as *soft decisions*). It will be shown that a careful design of the *supervisor* (also known as *fusion* strategy) yields a combined opinion which is more reliable than the best expert opinion.

4 System Model

Below is a list of the major notations we use throughout the paper, see also Figure 2.

i Index of the experts, $i \in 1 \ldots m$
j Index of the shots, $j \in 1 \ldots n, n+1$
x_{ij} Authenticity score delivered by expert i on shot j
s_{ij} Variance of x_{ij} as estimated by expert i
y_j The true authenticity score of shot j
z_{ij} The error score of an expert $z_{ij} = y_j - x_{ij}$

Note that the experts are allowed to provide a quality of the score which is modelled to be inversely proportional to s_{ij}. This strategy is novel with respect to the implemented supervisors reported so far in that it is the expert who is providing a variance on every authenticity score it delivers, not the supervisor. It is also worth pointing out that y_j can take only two numerical values corresponding to "False" and "True". If x_{ij} is between 0 and 1 then these values are chosen to be 0 and 1 respectively. We assume that the experts have been trained on other shots apart from $j \in 1 \ldots n, n + 1$. The supervisor is trained on shots $j \in 1 \ldots n$ (i.e. x_{ij} and y_j are known for $j \in 1 \ldots n$) and we consider shot $n + 1$ as a test shot on the working multimodal system (i.e. $x_{i,n+1}$ is known, but y_{n+1} is not known and the supervisor task is to estimate it).

5 Statistical Model

The model for combining the different experts is based on Bayesian statistics and the assumption of normal distributed expert errors, i.e. z_{ij} is considered to be a sample of the random variable $Z_{ij} \sim N(b_i, \sigma_{ij}^2)$. It has been shown experimentally [11] that this assumption does not strictly hold for common audio- and video-based biometric machine experts, but it is shown that it holds reasonably well when client and impostor distributions are considered separately. Taking this result into account, two different supervisors are constructed, one of them based on expert opinions where $y_j = 1$

$$\mathcal{C} = \{x_{ij}, s_{ij} | y_j = 1 \text{ and } 1 \leq j \leq n\} \qquad (1)$$

while the other is based on expert opinions where $y_j = 0$

$$\mathcal{I} = \{x_{ij}, s_{ij} | y_j = 0 \text{ and } 1 \leq j \leq n\} \qquad (2)$$

The two supervisors will be referred to as *client supervisor* and *impostor supervisor*, respectively (see Figure 2).

The client supervisor estimates the expected true authenticity score of an input claim based on its expertise on recognizing client data. More formally, it computes $M_{\mathcal{C}}'' = E[Y_{n+1} | \mathcal{C}, x_{i,n+1}]$ (the prime notation will become apparent later on). In case of impostor supervisor, $M_{\mathcal{I}}'' = E[Y_{n+1} | \mathcal{I}, x_{i,n+1}]$ is computed. The conciliated overall score M'' takes into account the different expertise of the two supervisors and chooses the one which came closest to its goal, i.e. 0 for the impostor supervisor and 1 for the client supervisor:

$$M'' = \begin{cases} M_{\mathcal{C}}'' & \text{if } |1 - M_{\mathcal{C}}''| - |0 - M_{\mathcal{I}}''| < 0 \\ M_{\mathcal{I}}'' & \text{otherwise} \end{cases} \qquad (3)$$

Based on the normality assumption of the errors, the supervisor algorithm described in [11] is obtained (see [13] for further background and details). In the following, we summarize this algorithm in the two cases where it can be applied.

5.1 Simplified Supervisor Algorithm

When no quality information is available, the following simplified supervisor algorithm is obtained by using $s_{ij} = 1$:

1. (Supervisor Training) Estimate the bias parameters of each expert. In case of the client supervisor the bias parameters are

$$M_{Ci} = \frac{1}{n_C} \sum_j z_{ij} \quad \text{and} \quad V_{Ci} = \frac{\alpha_{Ci}}{n_C} \tag{4}$$

where j indexes the training set C, n_C is the number of shots in C and

$$\alpha_{Ci} = \frac{1}{n_C - 3} \left(\sum_j z_{ij}^2 - \frac{1}{n_C} \left(\sum_j z_{ij} \right)^2 \right) \tag{5}$$

Similarly M_{Ii} and V_{Ii} are obtained for the impostor supervisor.

2. (Authentication Phase) At this step, both supervisors are operational, so that the time instant is always $n + 1$ and the supervisors have access to expert opinions $x_{i,n+1}$ but not access to the true authenticity score y_{n+1}. Client and impostor supervisors calibrate the experts according to their past performance, yielding (for the client supervisor)

$$M'_{Ci} = x_{i,n+1} + M_{Ci} \quad \text{and} \quad V'_{Ci} = (n_C + 1)V_{Ci} \tag{6}$$

and then the different calibrated experts are combined according to

$$M''_C = \frac{\sum_{i=1}^m \frac{M'_{Ci}}{V'_{Ci}}}{\sum_{i=1}^m \frac{1}{V'_{Ci}}} \tag{7}$$

Similarly, M'_{Ii}, V'_{Ii} and M''_I are obtained. The final supervisor opinion is obtained according to (3).

The algorithm described above has been successfully applied in [25] in a multimodal authentication system combining face and speech data. Verification performance improvements of almost an order magnitude were reported as compared to the best modality.

5.2 Full Supervisor Algorithm

When not only the experts scores but also the quality of the scores are available, the following algorithm is obtained:

1. (Supervisor Training) Estimate the bias parameters. For the client supervisor

$$M_{Ci} = \frac{\sum_j \frac{z_{ij}}{\sigma_{ij}^2}}{\sum_j \frac{1}{\sigma_{ij}^2}} \quad \text{and} \quad V_{Ci} = \frac{1}{\sum_j \frac{1}{\sigma_{ij}^2}} \tag{8}$$

where the training set $\mathcal{C}$ is used. The variances σ_{ij}^2 are estimated through $\bar{\sigma}_{ij}^2 = s_{ij} \cdot \alpha_{\mathcal{C}i}$, where

$$\alpha_{\mathcal{C}i} = \frac{1}{n_{\mathcal{C}} - 3} \left(\sum_j \frac{z_{ij}^2}{s_{ij}} - \left(\sum_j \frac{z_{ij}}{s_{ij}} \right)^2 \left(\sum_j \frac{1}{s_{ij}} \right)^{-1} \right) \qquad (9)$$

Similarly $M_{\mathcal{I}i}$ and $V_{\mathcal{I}i}$ are obtained for the impostor supervisor.

2. (Authentication Phase) First the supervisors calibrate the experts according to their past performance, for the client supervisor

$$M_{\mathcal{C}i}' = x_{i,n+1} + M_{\mathcal{C}i} \quad \text{and} \quad V_{\mathcal{C}i}' = s_{i,n+1}\alpha_{\mathcal{C}i} + V_{\mathcal{C}i} \qquad (10)$$

and then the different calibrated experts are combined according to (7). Similarly, $M_{\mathcal{I}i}'$, $V_{\mathcal{I}i}'$ and $M_{\mathcal{I}}''$ are obtained. The final supervisor opinion is obtained according to (3).

The algorithm described above has been successfully applied in [13] combining human expert opinions but not in a multimodal authentication application.

5.3   Adaptive Strategy

The variance s_{ij} of the score x_{ij} is provided by the expert and concerns a particular authentication assessment. It is not a general reliability measure for the expert itself, but a certainty measure based on qualitative knowledge of the expert and the data the expert assesses. Typically the variance of the score is chosen as the width of the range in which one can place the score. Because such intervals can be conveniently provided by a human expert, the algorithm in section 5.2 constitutes a systematic way of combining human and machine expertise in an authentication application. An example of such an application is forensics, where machine expert approaches have been proposed [26] and human opinions must be taken into consideration.

In this work, we propose to calculate s_{ij} for a machine expert by using a quality measure of the input biometric signal (see Figure 2). This implies taking into account equation (10) right, that the trained supervisor adapts the weights of the experts using the input signal quality. First we define the quality q_{ij} of the score x_{ij} according to

$$q_{ij} = \sqrt{Q_{ij} \cdot Q_{i,claim}} \qquad (11)$$

where Q_{ij} and $Q_{i,claim}$ are respectively the quality label of the biometric sample used by expert i in shot j and the average quality of the biometric samples used by expert i for modelling the claimed identity. The two quality labels Q_{ij} and $Q_{i,claim}$ are supposed to be in the range $[0, q_{max}]$ with $q_{max} > 1$ where 0 corresponds to the poorest quality, 1 corresponds to normal quality and q_{max} corresponds to the highest quality. Finally, the variance parameter is calculated according to

$$s_{ij} = \frac{1}{q_{ij}^2} \qquad (12)$$

6 Monomodal Experts

6.1 Speaker Expert

For the experiments reported in this work, the GMM-based speaker expert from Universidad Politecnica de Madrid used in the 2002 NIST Speaker Recognition evaluation [27] has been used. Below we briefly describe the basics, for more details we refer to [27, 28].

Feature extraction. Short-time analysis of the speech signal is carried out by using 20 ms Hamming windows shifted 10 ms. For each analysis window $t \in [1, 2, \ldots, T]$, a feature vector $\mathbf{m}_t$ based on Mel-Frequency Cepstral Coefficients (MFCC) and including first and second order time derivative approximations is generated. The feature vectors $M = \{\mathbf{m}_1, \mathbf{m}_2, \ldots, \mathbf{m}_T\}$ are supposed to be drawn from a user-dependent Gaussian Mixture Model λ which is estimated in the enrollment phase via MAP adaptation of a Universal Background Model λ_{UBM}. For our tests, the UBM is a text-independent 128 mixture GMM which was trained by using approximately 8 hours of Spanish mobile speech data (gender balanced).

Similarity computation. Given a test utterance parameterized as M and a claimed identity modeled as λ, a matching score x'_{ij} is calculated by using the log-likelihood ratio

$$x'_{ij} = \log\left(p\left[M|\lambda\right]\right) - \log\left(p\left[M|\lambda_{UBM}\right]\right) \tag{13}$$

Score normalization. In order to generate an expert opinion x_{ij} between 0 and 1, the matching score x'_{ij} is further normalized according to

$$x_{ij} = \frac{1}{1 + e^{-c \cdot x'_{ij}}} \tag{14}$$

The parameter c has been chosen heuristically on mobile speech data not used for the experiments reported here.

6.2 Fingerprint Expert

For the experiments reported in this work, the minutiae-based fingerprint expert described in [29] has been used. Below we describe the basics, for more details we refer to [29, 30].

Image enhancement. The fingerprint ridge structure is reconstructed according to: *i*) grayscale level normalization, *ii*) orientation field calculation, according to [31] *iii*) interest region extraction, *iv*) spatial-variant filtering according to the estimated orientation field, *v*) binarization, and *vi*) ridge profiling.

Fig. 3. Fingerprint feature extraction process

Similarity computation. Given a test and a reference minutiae pattern, a matching score x'_{ij} is computed. First, both patterns are aligned based on the minutia whose associated sampled ridge is most similar. The matching score is computed then by using a variant of the edit distance on polar coordinates and based on a size-adaptive tolerance box. When more than one reference minutiae pattern per client model are considered, the maximum matching score obtained by comparing the test and each reference pattern is used.

Score normalization. In order to generate an expert opinion x_{ij} between 0 and 1, the matching score x'_{ij} is further normalized according to

$$x_{ij} = \tanh\left(c \cdot x'_{ij}\right) \tag{15}$$

The parameter c has been chosen heuristically on fingerprint data not used for the experiments reported here.

7 Verification Performance Evaluation

Biometric verification can be considered as a detection task, involving a tradeoff between two type of errors: i) Type I error, also denoted as *False Rejection*

(FR) or miss (detection), occurring when a client, target, genuine, or authorized user is rejected by the system, and *ii*) Type II error, known as *False Acceptance* (FA) or false alarm, taking place when an unauthorized or impostor user is accepted as being a true user. Although each type of error can be computed for a given decision threshold, a single performance level is inadequate to represent the full capabilities of the system and, as such a system has many possible operating points, it is best represented by a complete performance curve. These total performance capabilities have been traditionally shown in form of ROC (Receiver -or also Relative- Operating Characteristic) plots, in which FA rate versus FR rate is depicted. A variant of this, the so-called DET (Detection Error Tradeoff) plot [33], is used here; in this case, the use of a normal deviate scale makes the comparison of competing systems easier. Moreover, the DET smoothing procedure introduced in [34], which basically consists in Gaussian Mixture Model estimation of FA and FR curves, has been also applied.

A specific point is attained when FAR and FRR coincide, the so-called EER (equal error rate); the global EER of a system can be easily detected by the intersection between the DET curve of the system and the diagonal line $y = x$. Nevertheless, and because of the step-like nature of FAR and FRR plots, EER calculation may be ambiguous according to the above-mentioned definition, so an operational procedure for computing the EER must be followed. In the present contribution, the procedure for computing the EER proposed in [35] has been applied.

8   Experiments

8.1   Database Description and Expert Protocol

Cellular speech data consist of short utterances in Spanish (the mobile number of each user). 75 users have been acquired, each one of them providing 10 utterance samples from 10 calls (within a month interval). The first 3 utterances are used as expert training data and the other 7 samples are used as expert test data. The recordings were carried out by a dialogue-driven computer-based acquisition process, and data were not further supervised. Moreover, 10 real impostor attempts per user are used as expert testing data, where each impostor knew the true mobile number and the way it was pronounced by the user he/she was forgering. Taking into account the automatic acquisition procedure and the highly skilled nature of the impostor data, near worst-case scenario has been prevailing in our experiments.

Fingerprint data from MCYT corpus has been used. For a detailed description of the contents and the acquisition procedure of the database, see [32]. Below, some information related to the experiments we have conducted is briefly described.

MCYT fingerprint subcorpus comprises 330 individuals acquired at 4 different Spanish academic sites by using high resolution capacitive and optical capture devices. For each user, the 10 prints were acquired under different acquisition conditions and levels of control. As a result, each individual provided a total number of 240 fingerprint images to the database (10 prints × 12 samples/print × 2 sensors/sample). Figure 4 shows three examples acquired with the optical scanner under the 3 considered levels of control.

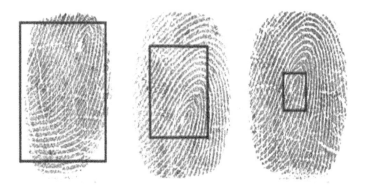

Fig. 4. Fingerprint images from MCYT corpus. Level of control from left to right: low, medium and high

Only the index fingers of the first 75 users in the database are used in the experiments. 10 print samples (optical scanner) per user are selected, 3 of them (each one from a different level of control) are used as expert training data and the other 7 are used as expert testing data. We have also considered a worst-case scenario using for each client the best 10 impostor fingerprint samples from a set of 750 different fingerprints.

All fingerprint images have been supervised and labelled according to the image quality by a human expert [29]. Basically, each different fingerprint image has been assigned a subjective quality measure from 0 (lowest quality) to 9 (highest quality) based on image factors like: incomplete fingerprint, smudge ridges or non uniform contrast, background noise, weak appearance of the ridge structure, significant breaks in the ridge structure, pores inside the ridges, etc. Figure 5 shows four example images and their labelled quality.

As a conclusion, each expert protocol comprises 75×7 client test attempts and 75×10 impostor test attempts in a near worst-case scenario.

8.2 Supervisor Protocol

Several methods have been described in the literature in order to maximize the use of the information in the training samples during a test [14]. For the error estimation in multimodal authentication systems, variants of the jackknife sampling using the leave-one-out principle are the common choice [23, 25]. In this work, and depending on the experiment at hand, one of the three following supervisor protocols has been used:

Fig. 5. Fingerprint images from MCYT corpus. Quality labelling from left to right: 0, 3, 6 and 9

Non-trained. All scores from client and impostor test attempts are used as supervisor test scores.

Trained-jacknife. One user is left out for supervisor testing, the supervisor training is carried out on the other users, the scheme is rotated for all the users and finally the errors are averaged.

Trained-bootstrap. N users are randomly selected with replacement for training, the testing is performed on the other users, the scheme is iterated B times and finally the errors are averaged.

8.3 Results

In the first experiment, we evaluate the verification performance of the three following fusion strategies: i) Sum Rule [12], which consists in averaging expert outputs; ii) The non-adaptive Bayesian Conciliation scheme [11] as described in section 5.1 (i.e. with $s_{ij} = 1$ for all authentication claims); and iii) The adaptive fusion strategy based on signal quality described in section 5.3. The non-trained supervisor protocol has been used for testing the Sum Rule approach whereas the trained-jacknife protocol has been followed for the other two trained fusion approaches. For the fingerprint expert, we have used the quality labels in MCYT database normalized into the range [0, 2]. For the speech expert $s_{ij} = 1$ is used. Trade-off verification results comparing the three fusion approaches are shown in Figure 6. As a result, any of the three fusion strategies clearly outperforms both the fingerprint (EER=4.55%) and the speaker expert (EER=4.32%). We also observe that the Sum Rule approach (EER=1.66%) is outperformed by the simplified Bayesian Conciliation scheme (EER=1.33%). The introduction of quality signals leads to further verification performance improvements in almost every working point (EER=0.94%).

In Figure 7, the client/impostor decision boundaries for one left-out user of the trained-jacknife supervisor protocol is depicted together with score maps

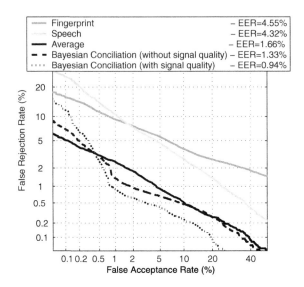

Fig. 6. Verification performance of fingerprint/speech experts and Sum/ Bayesian supervisors

of both training (background) and testing (enlarged) data. We note that the Sum Rule scheme does not take into account the actual client and impostor distributions, that is a skilled expert is weighted equally as a less skilled expert.

Some examples that may provide an intuitive idea about how the supervisor is adapted depending on the image quality of the input fingerprints are shown in Figure 8. We plot the decision boundaries for 2 different left-out users of the supervisor testing protocol together with score maps of both the training (background) and testing (enlarged) data. In the case the score quality is considered, we observe that the supervisor is adapted so as to increase or reduce the weight of the fingerprint expert opinion based on the fingerprint quality: the higher the image quality the higher the fingerprint expert weight and the lower the quality the lower the weight.

In the last experiment, we study the influence of an increasing number of clients N in the supervisor training set over the verification performance. In this case, the trained-bootstrap supervisor protocol with $B=200$ iterations has been used. As it is shown in Figure 9, the error rate decreases monotonically with the number of clients in the supervisor training set. In particular, a fast EER decay occurs for the first 10 clients and minor verification performance improvements are obtained for more than 20 users.

9   Conclusions

In this paper we have first summarized evidence that even one of the best known mono-modal recognition engines (human face recognition) is not able to reach a

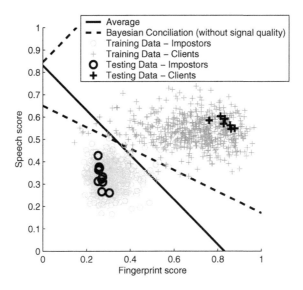

Fig. 7. Training/testing score maps and decision boundaries for Sum/Bayesian supervisors

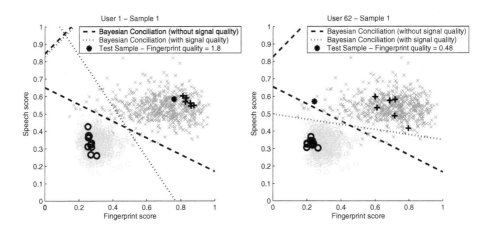

Fig. 8. Training/testing score maps and decision boundaries for Bayesian supervisors

recognition rate beyond 80 % when it is limited to a single view, i.e. a common approach in commercial applications. This has served as the motivation for, beginning with some common terminology and notations, the development of multi-modal automatic person authentication system models [11]. We have also explored an adaptive supervisor strategy and reviewed an implementation based

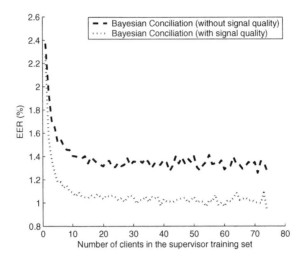

Fig. 9. Error rate vs number of clients in the supervisor training set

on signal quality of such a scheme [1]. The elements of a mobile authentication application based on speech and fingerprint data have been described and some experiments using this prototype on real data have been reported.

From the experiments, we conclude that multi-modal systems combining different biometric traits (EER=4.55% and EER=4.32% respectively for fingerprint and speaker experts in a near-worst case scenario) and using simple supervisor algorithms such as averaging can provide great benefits (EER=1.66%) in terms of verification error rates. Moreover, a Bayesian Conciliation fusion strategy have also been tested. In this case, it has been shown that weighting each expert output according to its past performance decreases error rates (EER=1.33%). Finally, we have also shown that the referenced adaptive fusion strategy can further improve the verification performance (EER=0.94%) compared to a trained but non-adaptive fusion strategy.

Future work includes the investigation of automatic quality measures for the different audio- and video-based biometric signals and the exploitation of the user-specific characteristics in the overall multi-modal authentication architecture.

10   Acknowledgements

In addition to Halmstad University, this work has been supported by the Spanish Ministry for Science and Technology under projects TIC2003-09068 and TIC2003-08382. J. F.-A. also thanks Consejeria de Educacion de la Comunidad de Madrid and Fondo Social Europeo for supporting his doctoral research.

References

[1] Bigun, J., Fierrez-Aguilar, J., Ortega-Garcia, J., Gonzalez-Rodriguez, J.: Multimodal biometric authentication using quality signals in mobile communications. In: Proc. of IAPR Intl. Conf. on Image Analysis and Processing, ICIAP, IEEE CS Press (2003) 2–13

[2] Baylis, G.C., Rolls, E., Leonard, C.M.: functional divisions of the temporal lobe neocortex. J. Neuroscience **7** (1987) 330–342

[3] Farah, M.J.: Is face recognition special? evidence from neuropsychology. Behavioral Brain Research **76** (1996) 181–189

[4] Elliott, E.S., Wills, E.J., Goldstein, A.G.: The effects of discrimination training on the recognition of white and oriental faces. Bulletin of the Psychonomic Society **2** (1973) 71–73

[5] Luce, T.S.: The role of experience in inter-racial recognition. Personality and Social Psychology Bulletin **1** (1974) 39–41

[6] Bothwell, R.K., Brigham, J.C., Malpass, R.S.: Cross-racial identification of faces. Personality and Social Psychology Bulletin **15** (1989) 19–25

[7] Bigun, J., Choy, K., Olsson, H.: Evidence on skill differences of women and men concerning face recognition. In Bigun, J., Smeraldi, F., eds.: Proc. of IAPR Intl. Conf. on Audio- and Video-based Person Authentication, AVBPA, Springer (2001) 44–51

[8] Kanade, T.: Picture processing system by computer complex and recognition of human faces. In: doctoral dissertation, Kyoto University. (1973)

[9] Atal, B.S.: Automatic recognition of speakers from their voices. Proceedings of the IEEE **64** (1976) 460–475

[10] Brunelli, R., Falavigna, D.: Person identification using multiple cues. IEEE Trans. Pattern Anal. and Machine Intell. **17** (1995) 955–966

[11] Bigun, E.S., Bigun, J., Duc, B., Fischer, S.: Expert conciliation for multi modal person authentication systems by bayesian statistics. In Bigun, J., Chollet, G., Borgefors, G., eds.: Proc. of IAPR Intl. Conf. on Audio- and Video-based Person Authentication, AVBPA, Springer (1997) 291–300

[12] Kittler, J., Hatef, M., Duin, R., Matas, J.: On combining classifiers. IEEE Trans. Pattern Anal. and Machine Intell. **20** (1998) 226–239

[13] Bigun, E.S.: Risk analysis of catastrophes using experts' judgments: An empirical study on risk analysis of major civil aircraft accidents in europe. European J. Operational Research **87** (1995) 599–612

[14] Duda, R.O., Hart, P.E., Stork, D.G.: Pattern classification. Wiley (2001)

[15] Ben-Yacoub, S., Abdeljaoued, Y., Mayoraz, E.: Fusion of face and speech data for person identity verification. IEEE Trans. on Neural Networks **10** (1999) 1065–1074

[16] Verlinde, P., Chollet, G., Acheroy, M.: Multi-modal identity verification using expert fusion. Information Fusion **1** (2000) 17–33

[17] Gutschoven, B., Verlinde, P.: Multi-modal identity verification using support vector machines (SVM). In: Proc. of the Intl. Conf. on Information Fusion, FUSION, IEEE Press (2000) 3–8

[18] Ross, A., Jain, A.K., Qian, J.Z.: Information fusion in biometrics. In Bigun, J., Smeraldi, F., eds.: Proc. of IAPR Intl. Conf. on Audio- and Video-based Person Authentication, AVBPA, Springer (2001) 354–359

[19] Kittler, J., Messer, K.: Fusion of multiple experts in multimodal biometric personal identity verification systems. In: Proc. of the IEEE Workshop on Neural Networks for Signal Processing, NNSP. (2002) 3–12

[20] Duin, R.P.W.: The combining classifier: to train or not to train? In: Proc. of the IAPR Intl. Conf. on Pattern Recognition, ICPR, IEEE CS Press (2002) 765–770

[21] Roli, F., Fumera, G., Kittler, J.: Fixed and trained combiners for fusion of imbalanced pattern classifiers. In: Proc. of the Intl. Conf. on Information Fusion, FUSION. (2002) 278–284

[22] Jain, A.K., Ross, A.: Learning user-specific parameters in a multibiometric system. In: Proc. of the IEEE Intl. Conf. on Image Processing, ICIP. Volume 1. (2002) 57–60

[23] Fierrez-Aguilar, J., Ortega-Garcia, J., Garcia-Romero, D., Gonzalez-Rodriguez, J.: A comparative evaluation of fusion strategies for multimodal biometric verification. In: Proc. of IAPR Intl. Conf. on Audio- and Video-based Person Authentication, AVBPA, Springer (2003) 830–837

[24] Ellis, H.D., Ellis, D.M., Hosie, J.A.: Priming effects in childrens face recognition. British Journal of Psychology **84** (1993) 101–110

[25] Bigun, J., Duc, B., Fischer, S., Makarov, A., Smeraldi, F.: Multi modal person authentication. In et. al., H.W., ed.: Nato-Asi advanced study on face recogniton. Volume F-163., Springer (1997) 26–50

[26] Gonzalez-Rodriguez, J., Fierrez-Aguilar, J., Ortega-Garcia, J.: Forensic identification reporting using automatic speaker recognition systems. In: Proc. of the IEEE Intl. Conf. on Acoustics, Speech and Signal Processing, ICASSP. Volume 2. (2003) 93–96

[27] Garcia-Romero, D., et al.: ATVS-UPM results and presentation at NIST"2002 speaker recognition evaluation (2002)

[28] Reynolds, D.A., Quatieri, T.F., Dunn, R.B.: Speaker verification using adapted gaussian mixture models. Digital Signal Processing **10** (2000) 19–41

[29] Simon-Zorita, D., Ortega-Garcia, J., Fierrez-Aguilar, J., Gonzalez-Rodriguez, J.: Image quality and position variability assessment in minutiae-based fingerprint verification. IEE Proceedings Vision, Image and Signal Processing **150** (2003)

[30] Jain, A.K., Hong, L., Pankanti, S., Bolle, R.: An identity authentication system using fingerprints. Proceedings of the IEEE **85** (1997) 1365–1388

[31] Bigun, J., Granlund, G.H.: Optimal orientation detection of linear symmetry. In: First International Conference on Computer Vision, ICCV (London), Washington, DC., IEEE Computer Society Press (1987) 433–438

[32] Ortega-Garcia, J., et al.: MCYT baseline corpus: A bimodal biometric database. IEE Proceedings Vision, Image and Signal Processing **150** (2003)

[33] Martin, A., Doddington, G., Kamm, T., Ordowski, M., Przybocki, M.: The DET curve in assessment of decision task performance. In: Proc. of ESCA Eur. Conf. on Speech Comm. and Tech., EuroSpeech. (1997) 1895–1898

[34] Garcia-Romero, D., Fierrez-Aguilar, J., Gonzalez-Rodriguez, J., Ortega-Garcia, J.: Support vector machine fusion of idiolectal and acoustic speaker information in spanish conversational speech. In: Proc. of the IEEE Intl. Conf. on Acoustics, Speech and Signal Processing, ICASSP. Volume 2. (2003) 229–232

[35] Maio, D., Maltoni, D., Cappelli, R., Wayman, J.L., , Jain, A.K.: FVC2000: fingerprint verification competition. IEEE Trans. Pattern Anal. and Machine Intell. **24** (2002) 402–412

Biometric Gait Recognition

Jeffrey E. Boyd[1] and James J. Little[2]

[1] Department of Computer Science
University of Calgary
boyd@cpsc.ucalgary.ca
[2] Department of Computer Science
University of British Columbia
little@cs.ubc.ca

Abstract. Psychological studies indicate that people have a small but statistically significant ability to recognize the gaits of individuals that they know. Recently, there has been much interest in machine vision systems that can duplicate and improve upon this human ability for application to biometric identification. While gait has several attractive properties as a biometric (it is unobtrusive and can be done with simple instrumentation), there are several confounding factors such as variations due to footwear, terrain, fatigue, injury, and passage of time. This paper gives an overview of the factors that affect both human and machine recognition of gaits, data used in gait and motion analysis, evaluation methods, existing gait and quasi gait recognition systems, and uses of gait analysis beyond biometric identification. We compare the reported recognition rates as a function of sample size for several published gait recognition systems.

1 Introduction

People often feel that they can identify a familiar person from afar simply by recognizing the way the person walks. This common experience, combined with recent interest biometrics, has lead to the development of gait recognition as a from of biometric identification.

As a biometric, gait has several attractive properties. Acquisition of images portraying an individual's gait can be done easily in public areas, with simple instrumentation, and does not require the cooperation or even awareness of the individual under observation. In fact, it seems that it is the possibility that a subject may not be aware of the surveillance and identification that raises public concerns about gait biometrics [1].

There are also several confounding properties of gait as a biometric. Unlike finger prints, we do not know the extent to which an individual's gait is unique. Furthermore, there are several factors, other than the individual, that cause variations in gait, including footwear, terrain, fatigue, and injury.

This paper gives an overview of the factors that affect both human and machine recognition of gaits, data used in gait and motion analysis, evaluation methods, existing gait and quasi gait recognition systems, and uses of gait analysis beyond biometric identification.

M. Tistarelli, J. Bigun, and E. Grosso (Eds.): Biometrics School 2003, LNCS 3161, pp. 19–42, 2005.
© Springer-Verlag Berlin Heidelberg 2005

1.1   Gait and Gait Recognition

We define gait to be *the coordinated, cyclic combination of movements that result in human locomotion*. The movements are coordinated in the sense that they must occur with a specific temporal pattern for the gait to occur. The movements in a gait repeat as a walker cycles between steps with alternating feet. It is both the *coordinated* and *cyclic* nature of the motion that makes gait a unique phenomenon.

Examples of motion that are gaits include walking, running, jogging, and climbing stairs. Sitting down, picking up an object, and throwing and object are coordinated motions, but they are not cyclic. Jumping jacks are coordinated and cyclic, but do not result in locomotion.

Therefore, we define gait recognition to be the recognition of some salient property, e.g., identity, style of walk, or pathology, based on the coordinated, cyclic motions that result in human locomotion. In the case of biometric gait recognition, the salient property is identity. We make the distinction between gait recognition and what we call quasi gait recognition in which a salient property is recognized based on features acquired while a subject is walking, but the features are not inherently part of the gait. For example, skeletal dimensions may be measured during gait and used to recognize an individual. However, skeletal dimensions may be measured other ways, and are therefore not a property of the gait.

1.2   Human Perception of Gait

The ability of humans to recognize gaits has long been of interest to psychologists. Johansson [2, 3] showed that humans can quickly (in less than one second) identify that a pattern of moving lights, called a moving light display (MLD), corresponds to a walking human. However, when presented with a static image from the MLD, humans are unable to recognize any structure at all. For example, without knowing that the dots in a single frame of the sequence shown in Fig. 1 are on the joints of a walking figure, it is difficult to recognize them as such. What we cannot show in a print medium is, that within a fraction of a second after the dots move, one can recognize them as being from a human gait.

Johansson's contributions are important because they provide an experimental method that allows one to view motion extracted from other contextual information. With the context removed, the importance of motion becomes obvious. Johansson also suggests a set of gestalt rules that humans use to connect the moving dots and infer structure.

Bertenthal and Pinto [4] identify the following three important properties in the human perception of gaits.

- *Frequency entrainment.* The various components of the gait must share a common frequency.

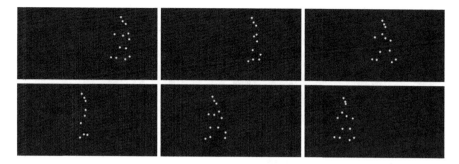

Fig. 1. Frames from a moving light display of a person walking. People can quickly identify that the motion is a gait from the moving sequence, but have difficulty with static frames.

– *Phase locking.* The phase relationships among the components of the gait remain approximately constant. The lock varies for different types of locomotion such as walking versus running.
– *Physical plausibility.* The motion must be physically plausible human motion.

As shown in Fig. 2, there are motions at different frequencies within a gait. However, the gait has a fundamental frequency that corresponds to the complete cycle. Other frequencies are multiples of the fundamental. This is frequency entrainment. It is not possible to walk with component motions at arbitrary frequencies.

When the motions are at entrained frequencies, the phase of the motions must be locked, i.e., the timing patterns of the motions are fixed. In a typical gait, the left arms swings in phase with the right leg and opposite in phase with the left leg, a pattern that is fixed throughout the gait. This is phase locking.

To understand physical plausibility, consider the motion of the star of an action movie such as Jackie Chan or Jet Li. On occasion, the actors will use wires to allow them to perform feats that would not be physically possible otherwise. However, even though the wires are not visible in the movie, viewers know that the wires are there because the motion is not physically plausible without them. Currently, physical plausibility is not employed in machine analysis of gait, other than by the use of exemplars which are real, and therefore physically plausible.

It appears that there is a special connection between human gaits and human perception. Cohen et al. [5] observed that while humans can easily recognize human motion, they have more difficulty recognizing animal motion. Cohen et al. explain this observation by suggesting that humans rely on the same mechanisms that they use to generate their own gait to perceive the gaits of others. If correct, this may indicate how to improve machine perception of gait.

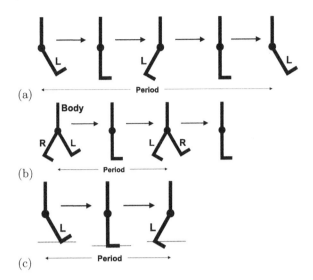

Fig. 2. Stylized body and legs showing sources of different frequencies in a synthesized gait: (a) the oscillation of a swinging limb repeats periodically, e.g., left foot fall to left foot fall, (b) the silhouette of a body repeats at twice that frequency, i.e., step to step, and (c) the pendulum motion of limbs has vertical motion at twice the frequency of the limbs horizontal motion.

1.3   Important Factors in Evaluation of Gait Analysis Systems

There are many and varied approaches to gait analysis. In order to interpret them in some common context, we suggest the following approach to understanding gait analysis systems.

1. Identify the oscillating signals that the system derives from the cyclic motion.
2. Determine how the oscillating signals establish frequency entrainment, phase locking, and physical plausibility.
3. Determine how the oscillating signals translate into features that can be used for recognition.

2   Potential for Gait as a Biometric

The use of gait as a biometric for human identification is still young when compared to methods that use voice, finger prints, or faces. Thus, it is not yet clear how useful gait is for biometrics. In this section we consider evidence from several sources, including known properties of the human body and human performance to gain insight.

2.1   Optimistic Viewpoint

Bhanu and Han [6] present an optimistic view of the potential for biometric gait recognition. Their analysis is built upon a gait recognition system that measures a subject's skeletal dimensions as he walks. Therefore, it is possible to estimate an upper bound on the performance of the system from known distributions of skeletal dimensions in a human population. They compute their estimate using a Monte Carlo simulation seeded with the population statistics and a set of assumptions about the accuracy of the skeletal dimension measurements. Plots showing the bounds they compute are in Fig. 8.

Since theirs is a quasi gait recognition system, it is reasonable to ask whether or not the bound might reasonably apply to gait recognition too. Do skeletal dimensions sufficiently constrain a gait for the purposes of recognition? The answer is unknown, but work in mechanical engineering can shed some light. McGeer [7, 8], and later Coleman and Ruina [9], Garcia et al. [10], and Collins et al. [11] have demonstrated passive mechanical walkers. These are mechanical machines that oscillate without external force to produce a gait as the machine *falls* down an incline. This implies that gait is a natural bi-product of the structure of the human body, and the mass and skeletal dimensions of the body are what determine the oscillations that produce the gait. Thus, to a large extent, Bhanu and Han are right to equate skeletal dimensions with gait. However, mass and other factors contribute to a human gait.

It is worth noting here that many gait analysis systems could benefit from the definition of a *standard* or *normal* gait. Passive mechanical walkers have the potential to define such a gait because they show the innate gait of the kinematic structure in the absence of muscular forces.

Bhanu and Han's results show one important feature of gait and other biometric systems. Regardless of the quality of biometric, the system performance in terms of recognition rate drops with increased population size. The best that one can hope for is that the rate at which performance drops is tolerable.

2.2   Human Performance

People often have the impression that they can recognize friends by their gaits. Although this ability has been confirmed by experiments using MLDs, human ability to recognize people from motion is limited.

For example, Barclay et al. [12], and Kozlowski and Cutting [13] showed that humans can recognize the gender of a walker from an MLD. However, for short exposures to the MLD (two seconds or less), humans were no better than random. It required longer exposures, on the order of four seconds, for humans to perform better than random. Even at that, the recognition rate was 66% when random was 50%.

Cutting and Kozlowski [14] also showed that people can recognize their friends from MLDs. Again, this result needs clarification. The experiment involved six students who knew each other well. Experimenters recorded MLDs for the six students. Then, at a later date, the original six, plus a seventh who was also a friend, tried to recognize their friends from the MLDs. The correct recognition rate was 38% which is significantly better than random (17%). Thus, the conclusion that people can recognize friends from motion is correct, but not well enough to be a reliable form of identification. It seems that people rely on other contextual clues more than they realize.

2.3   Confounding Factors

If passive mechanical walkers are a good indication, then the primary determinant of a gait is a person's skeletal dimensions and mass. Other factors play a role too, including:

- **terrain** (Laszlo et al. [15] illustrate variations in human gait due to terrain in computer graphic),
- **injury** (Murray et al. [16] and Murray [17] describe the effects of injury on gait),
- **footwear**, (von Tscharner [18] shows that muscle activation in walkers changes when people walk bare foot as opposed to wearing shoes),
- **muscle development**,
- **fatigue**,
- **training** (athletic training or military marching drills),
- **cultural artifacts** (e.g., mince, swagger, and strut), and
- **personal idiosyncrasies**.

Each of these factors may confound biometric gait recognition.

3   Data in Gait Recognition

In this section we give an overview of the types of data used in gait and motion analysis systems.

3.1   Background Subtraction

Background subtraction is a method for identifying moving objects against a static background. Although there are many variations on the theme, the basic idea is to

1. estimate the pixel properties of the static background,
2. subtract actual pixel values from the background estimates, and
3. assume that if the difference exceeds a given threshold that the pixel must be part of a moving object.

Normally one follows the last step by forming connected components, or blobs, of moving pixels that correspond to the moving objects. Factors that confound background subtraction include background motion, moving objects that are similar in appearance to the background, background variations over long periods of time, and objects in close proximity merging together. In general, the variations on the theme of background subtraction involve selecting pixel properties to compare, background models, and innovations to address any number of confounding factors. Examples include Hunter et al. [19], Horprasert et al. [20], Stauffer and Grimson [21], and Javed et al. [22].

Fig. 3 shows an example of background subtraction taken from the MoBo database [23].

(a)   (b)

Fig. 3. Example of background subtraction from MoBo database [23]: (a) original image (deliberately blurred to conceal the subject's identity), and (b) segmented image.

3.2 Silhouettes

Background subtraction provides a set of pixels within the region of a moving object. Alternatively, one may only be interested in the outline of that region. We refer to this outline as a silhouette. An examples of gait analysis that uses silhouettes is in Baumberg and Hogg [24].

3.3 Optical Flow

A motion field, is a projection of motion in a scene onto the image plane. Optical flow refers to the movement or flow of pixel brightness in an image sequence, and is a quantity that we can estimate from images sequences. Although the motion field and optical flow are not the same, we often use optical flow as an approximation to the motion field since most flow is caused by observed motion.

Barron, Jepson and Fleet [25] provide an excellent overview of several optical flow algorithms that compares their performance. They divide the algorithms into four categories: differential, region-matching, energy-based, and phase-based. We will consider only the first two categories since they are the most popular.

Differential flow algorithms find solutions to a differential equation, the optical flow constraint equation [26],

$$I_x u + I_y v + I_t = 0$$

where I is the spatiotemporal (x, y, and t) image sequence, I_x, I_y, I_t are the partial derivatives of I with respect to space and time, and u and v are the x and y image velocities, i.e., the optical flow. Fig. 4 shows a sample frame of optical flow computed using the Lucas and Kanade [27] least-squares algorithm for differential flow.

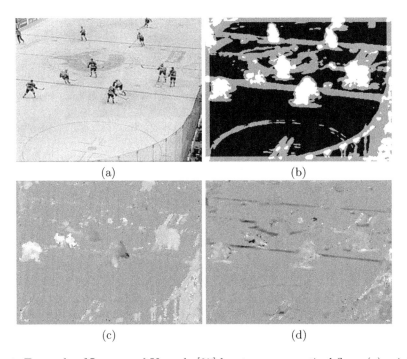

(a)   (b)

(c)   (d)

Fig. 4. Example of Lucas and Kanade [27] least squares optical flow: (a) original image from a sequence, (b) validity map, and (c) x- and (d) y-direction optical flow. In (b) black, gray and white mean no flow, gradient flow and least-squares flow respectively. In (c) and (d) gray is zero, black is negative (left/up), and white is positive (right/down).

Region-matching optical flow algorithms compute flow by comparing regions in consecutive images of a sequence. When regions match, the algorithms conclude that the region has moved and sets the flow accordingly. Fig. 5 shows an example of optical flow computed using the region-matching algorithm of Bulthoff et al. [28].

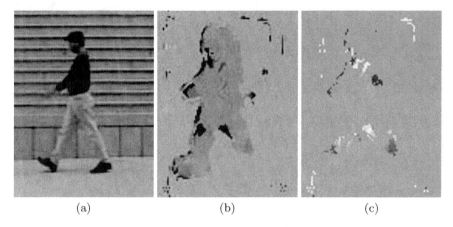

(a)   (b)   (c)

Fig. 5. Example of Bulthoff et al. [28] region-matching optical flow: (a) original image from a sequence, and (b) x- and (c) y-direction optical flow. In (b) and (c) gray is zero, black is negative (left/up), and white is positive (right/down).

3.4   Motion Energy and Motion History Images

Davis and Bobick [29] describe a motion energy image (MEI) and a motion history image (MHI), both derived from temporal image sequences. In the MEI, image pixels indicate whether or not there has been any motion at that pixel in previous frames. Note that an MEI cannot indicate in what order the pixels experienced the motion and therefore cannot encapsulate timing patterns in a motion. The MHI addresses this by indicating how recently motion occurred at each pixel. The brighter the region in an MHI, the more recent the motion. Fig. 6 shows images and the MHI from a sample sequence. Davis and Bobick [29] show that shapes in the MEI and MHI can be used to recognize various activities.

4   Evaluation of Gait Biometrics

4.1   Evaluation Methods

Typically, gait biometrics are tested in a recognition system like that shown in Fig. 7. The system extracts a set of descriptive features for an unknown test subject. It then compares the features to those of known subjects stored in a database. This model is adequate for evaluation of recognition and surveillance situations where there is no prior information provided about the identity of the subject.

Fig. 6. Example of a motion history image (MHI) [29]. The leftmost three images show the the motion sequence while the image on the right is the resulting MHI.

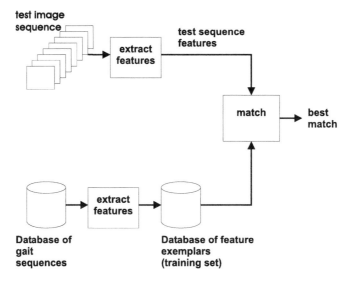

Fig. 7. Typical system for testing performance of gait recognition and other biometric systems.

Two broad approaches to evaluation have emerged. The first is to estimate the rate of correct recognition, while the second is to compare the variations in a population versus the variations in measurements. Neither method is entirely satisfactory, but they both provide insights into performance. We discuss both roaches in the remainder of this section.

4.2   Recognition Rate

Estimating the rate of correct recognition for a gait biometric has an intuitive appeal. It seems natural to think of system performance in terms of how often the system *gets it right*.

To arrive at such estimates, the procedure is to take a sample of the population of interest. One then divides the sample into two partitions, one for training the system (the database in Fig. 7), and one for testing. The estimated rate of correct recognition is the fraction of the test set that the system classifies correctly.

Such an estimate is extremely sensitive to context. Variations in any of the following factors will affect the resulting estimate.

- **Randomization of sample:** For the estimate to have any relevance outside the experiment, the sample must be a randomly selected from the population of interest. Such sampling is time-consuming and expensive. Consequently, most estimates produced in research are based on a biased sample that reflects mostly graduate. Campbell and Stanley [30] give one of the most thorough treatments of experimental design and the need for randomization.
- **Randomization of partitions:** It is essential that the training and test partitions be selected at random. Failure to do this can introduce a bias into the estimate. Cohen [31] gives excellent descriptions of methods for cross validation that avoid such biases.
- **Sampling conditions:** It is time-consuming to acquire samples over extended periods of time, and over a variety of imaging conditions. Thus, current samples are biased toward conditions in a single session using a single imaging apparatus. When researchers have reported results for samples that span weeks to months, e.g., Tanawongsuwan and Bobick [32], recognition rates drop drastically when compared to samples acquired in a single session.
- **Sample size:** Recognition rates drop with increases in sample size. For example, see the trends in the plots in Bhanu and Han [6] and Ben-Abdelkader et al. [33]. Intuitively, this occurs because the larger the sample, the more opportunities there are to make a mistake. In terms of the features used for recognition, as the sample size increases, the feature space becomes crowded, thus providing less resolution between individuals.

In spite of their intuitive appeal, recognition rates must be considered only within the context in which they are produced. Failure to consider any of the above factors in comparing recognition rates will almost certainly lead to false conclusions.

4.3   Analysis of Variance

While there is no way to avoid the issues of sample randomization, partition randomization, and sampling conditions, there are methods for dealing with variations in sample size. Consider the f statistic,

$$f = \frac{MS_{between}}{MS_{within}},$$

where $MS_{between}$ and MS are the mean-square errors between classes (between individuals) and within classes (for a single individual) due to the accumulation of all factors that cause a gait and its measured features to vary. When f is large, individuals are spread widely throughout the feature space with respect to the variations for an individual. When $f = 1$, then individuals are indistinguishable. A large f does not eliminate the trend toward lower recognition rates with sample size, but it does reduce the rate at which recognition deteriorates.

The f statistic is the foundation of analysis of variance (ANOVA) [34]. ANOVA is a method of hypothesis testing that uses the known distribution of f under the condition that classes/individuals are indistinguishable, also referred to as the null hypothesis. If a sample produces a value of f that is large enough, one rejects the null hypothesis and concludes that there is significant variation between classes. Note that sample size is a parameter of the known distributions of f f may be interpreted for samples of different size. Bobick and Johnson [35] describe *expected confusion*, $E[A]$, a number that is directly related to f ($E[A] = 1/\sqrt{f}$), and its role in predicting performance for varying sample size.

While f address issues of sample size, it is not clear how to compare f for different feature spaces, especially when data can be linear, as in a persons height, or directional, as in the phase of a signal. Directional ANOVA exists [36], but is it correct to compare the values of f directly. Furthermore, the distribution of f can depend on the dimensionality of the feature space. Currently, f appears to be a useful way to compare results acquired with different sample sizes, but it needs further development.

5   Existing Gait Recognition Systems

In this section, we describe and compare a selection of biometric gait recognition systems. As the previous section suggested, it is difficult to compare different systems directly when each is tested with a different sample. To address this issue here, in Fig. 8 we plot the recognition rate versus sample size for the methods that report recognition rates. Note that this does not adequately address all the issues of sampling, but serves only to provide an approximate picture of the *state-of-the-art* in gait recognition.

In the following subsections, we categorize the methods by their source of oscillations: shape, joint trajectory, self similarity, and pixel.

5.1   Shape Oscillations

Fig. 9 shows the *shape-of-motion* system developed by Little and Boyd [37]. The system uses optical flow to identify a moving figure in a sequence of images. It then describes the shape of the moving figure with a set of scalars derived from Cartesian moments. For example, the descriptors include the x and y coordinates of the object centroid, the x and y coordinates of the object centroid

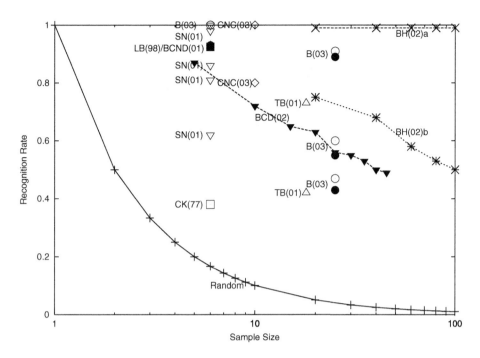

Fig. 8. Performance comparison of biometric gait recognition systems showing recognition rate versus sample size. The curve labeled **Random** indicates the expected recognition rate for random guesses. **CK(77)** refers to Cutting and Kozlowski [14], **BH(02)a** and **BH(02)b** refer to Bhanu and Han [6] 5mm and 40mm resolution respectively, **LB(98)** refers to Little and Boyd [37], **BCND(01)** refers to Ben-Abdelkader et al. [38], **SN(01)** refers to Shutler and Nixon [39], **TB(01)** refers to Tanawongsuwan and Bobick [32], **CNC(03)** refers to Cunado et al. [40], **B(03)** refers to Boyd [41], and **BCD(02)** refers to Ben-Abdelkader et al. [33].

weighted by the magnitude of the optical flow, and the aspect ratio of the distribution of pixels. When taken over the duration of the sequence, each scalar forms a time series. The shape-of-motion system extracts the oscillations from each series, then finds the frequency and phase of the oscillations, thus performing frequency entrainment and phase locking. The result is a set of m phases, one per scalar. The system takes one phase as a reference, then subtracts the reference to produce a feature vector of $m - 1$ phases. In their evaluation, Little and Boyd achieved a recognition rate of approximately 92% for a sample size of six.

Shutler and Nixon [39] extend the shape-of-motion concept to use Zernike *velocity moments* to compute shape descriptions over an entire sequence, rather than on a frame by frame basis. They test their system on the shape-of-motion [37]

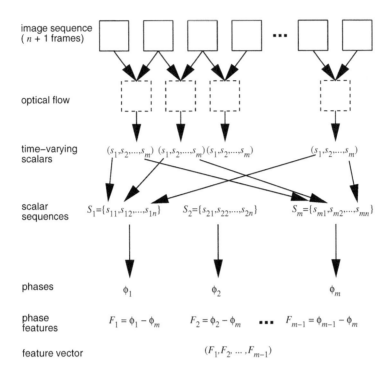

Fig. 9. The shape-of-motion gait recognition system [37].

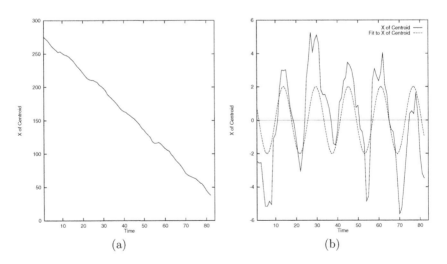

(a)   (b)

Fig. 10. Sample data from the shape-of-motion system: (a) a x-   rdinate sequence, and (b) the sequence with the non-oscillatory component removed and
a fitted sinusoid at the measured frequency and phase.

database, achieving recognition rates in the range of 62% to 100%, depending upon which velocity moments they include in their feature vector, for a sample size of six.

5.2   Joint Trajectory Patterns

Tanawongsuwan and Bobick (2001) [32] use joint angle trajectories measured using a magnetic-marker motion-capture system. As such, theirs is not a vision system and would not be practical for biometrics, but it does indicate the potential for joint angle trajectory features, if they were to be measured by some other means. They estimate the frequency of the gait and align the left and right, hip and knee joint trajectories to a common point in the gait cycle. They also resample the sequences to a common length. These steps effectively perform frequency entrainment and phase locking. The set of four trajectories combine to form one large feature vector used for recognition.

Tanawongsuwan and Bobick evaluated their system on a sample size of 18 and achieved a recognition rate of 73%. They further tested their system using an additional eight test sequences captured at a later date. When recognizing this latter sample using training data from the first sample, the recognition rate dropped to 42%. This demonstrates the deterioration in performance that occurs when samples span long periods of time.

Cunado et al. [40] extract a hip joint trajectory from a sequence of images. They acquire a trajectory for the hip closest to the camera only. They then use Fourier components of the trajectory as features for recognition. A test of their method on a database of size 10 yields recognition rates of 80% and 100% for Fourier features, and phase-weighted Fourier features respectively. Given the significance of phase locking in human perception of gaits, it is not surprising that the inclusion of phase information in the feature vector improves the recognition rate.

5.3   Temporal Patterns in Self-Similarity

As a person walks, the configuration of their body repeats periodically. For this reason, images in a gait sequence tend to be similar to other images in the sequence when separated in time by the period of the gait (the time between left foot strikes) and half the period (the time between left and right foot strikes). Fig. 11 illustrates this point.

Ben-Abdelkader et al. [38] exploit this *self similarity* to create a representation of gait sequences that is useful for gait recognition. From an image sequence, they construct a self-similarity image in which pixel intensities indicate the extent to which two images in the sequence are alike, i.e., pixel (i, j) in the self-similarity image indicates the similarity of the images at times t_i and t_j. With a cyclic motion such as a gait, the self-similarity image has a repeating texture. The frequency of the gait determines the rate at which the texture repeats (and thus is a form of frequency entrainment). Furthermore, variations in the timing of motions between individuals become details in the self-similarity

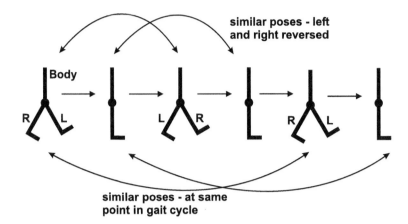

Fig. 11. Self similarity in gait sequences. Images separated by a full or half period of the gait tend to be alike.

image texture (and thus is a form of phase locking). Self-similarity images are large, so Ben-Abdelkader et al. use a principal component analysis on the space of similarity images to create a lower-dimensional eigenspace of images. The projections of self-similarity images onto this eigenspace become features for gait recognition.

Ben-Abdelkader et al. [38] test their system on the shape-of-motion database [37] and achieve a recognition rate of 93% with a sample size of six.

5.4   Pixel Oscillations

When a walker appears to be stationary in an image sequence, either as a result of tracking or walking on a treadmill, the cyclic motions of the gait result in intensity oscillations in pixels. The frequency of the gait and the timing of the component motions determine the frequency and phase of the pixel oscillations. Boyd [42] demonstrated that an array of phase-locked loops (PLL), one per pixel, can synchronize internal oscillators to the frequency and phase of pixel oscillations. This synchronization process inherently performs frequency entrainment and phase locking.

Boyd uses a phasor (Fig. 12), a complex number that represents a rotating vector, to represent the magnitude and phase of the oscillations at each pixel. Thus, once the PLL synchronization occurs, one can construct a complex image of phasors in which each pixel indicates the extent to which there are oscillations and the relative timing of the oscillations (Fig. 13). Procrustes shape analysis [43, 36] (Fig. 14) is a method for the statistical comparison of shapes represented as complex vectors. Thus, Procrustes shape analysis provides an ideal method to compare vectors of phasors that represent image oscillations.

Fig. 12. A phasor, or phase vector, is a complex vector that rotates about the origin, generating a sinusoid when projected onto the real axis. The magnitude and direction of the vector gives the amplitude and phase of the sinusoid respectively. Timing is given by the relative phases. Here phasor **A** leads phasor **B**.

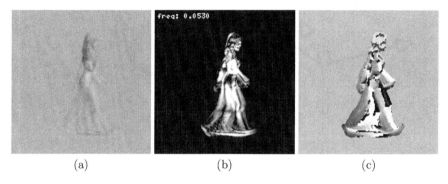

Fig. 13. Sample output of phase-locked loops: (a) superposition of frames from the input sequence, (b) magnitude of oscillations, and (c) phase of oscillations (note the phase wrap that results from the display of phase as a gray level).

Boyd [41] tested the phase-locked loops for the ability to recognize individual people using the shape-of-motion database [37] and the MoBo database [23]. With shape-of-motion data, recognition was perfect, 100% with sample size six. Using the MoBo database recognition rates were between 47% and 91% depending on whether or not sequences portraying the same style of gait were allowed to match. Boyd also observed that ignoring the phase information lowered the recognition rate in all cases.

In related work, Liu and Picard [44] Polana and Nelson [45] also look pixel level variations to analyze cyclic motions, however, they do not apply their analysis to biometric recognition. See Sec. 6 for more details.

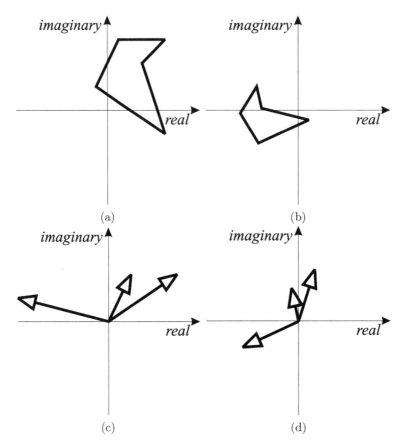

Fig. 14. Procrustes analysis applied to shape and phase configurations. In the conventional application, a shape is represented by a vector of complex vertices. The shape in (a), is the same as the shape (b) because each one is a translated, scaled, and rotated version of the other. A phasor configuration is also a vector of complex numbers. The configuration in (c) is the same as that in (d) because each one is a rotated and scaled version of the other. Rotation is always about the origin so translation can be ignored.

6   Other Systems

The methods described in this section are related to gait recognition, but are not mentioned in Sec. 5 because they are either quasi gait methods, not specific to gait, or do not do recognition. This is not to say that these methods are inferior, but that we merely choose to classify them differently.

6.1   Quasi Gait Recognition

Biometric recognition methods that do not rely on properties unique to a gait, but make measurements of a person during a gait, we refer to as quasi gait methods. One advantage to quasi gait approaches is that they may be less sensitive to variation in a gait. For example, a person's gait may vary for reasons discussed, but their skeletal dimensions will remain constant. Examples of quasi gait methods are discussed here.

Bobick and Johnson [35] measure a set of four parameters that describe a static pose extracted from a gait sequence. These parameters are height, torso length, leg length, and stride length, all of which can be estimated from a single image (see Fig. 15). Bobick and Johnson then use these parameters as feature vectors for recognition. The authors evaluate their method using *expected confusion*, a number related to the f statistic. For this reason we are unable to compare their results in the plot of Fig. 8.

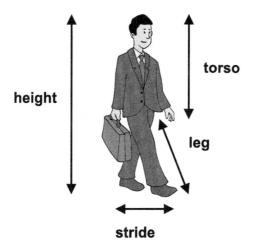

Fig. 15. Static gait features measured by Bobick and Johnson [35]: height, torso length, leg length, and stride length.

Ben-Abdelkader et al. [33] extract a subject's height, amplitude of height oscillations during gait, gait cadence, and stride length (see Fig. 16). They then use these values in a feature vector for recognition. Although the features include cadence, the method uses no timing information from the gait so we classify it as quasi gait recognition. Using the full feature set, they achieved a recognition rate of 49% with a sample size of 45, acquired over two days. They also look at subsamples to determine the rate at which performance deteriorated with sample size. The results are plotted in Fig. 8.

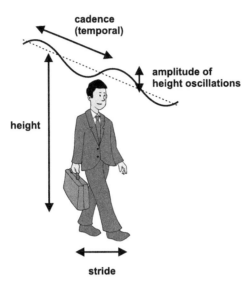

Fig. 16. Gait features measured by Ben-Abdelkader et al. [33]: mean height, amplitude of height oscillations, stride length and cadence.

It should be noted that these methods require some camera calibration and knowledge of the distance from camera to subject. This is done to obtain measurements in real-world units that can be measured with varying apparatus at different times.

6.2   Non-recognition Systems

Methods in this section either do not do gait recognition specifically, or do not do recognition at all.

Polana and Nelson [45] examine oscillations in the magnitude of the optical flow in a sequence containing periodic motion. They compute a coarse resolution (four by four) flow magnitude image at six points in the period of the motion. From this they form a 96-element vector that is used to recognize a broad range of periodic motions, but not individual gaits.

Liu and Picard [44] examine oscillations in pixel intensity for a gait sequence using fast Fourier transforms (FFT). Their analysis identifies the amplitude of the fundamental frequency of the gait. They did not use phase in their analysis, nor did they do recognition.

Baumberg and Hogg [46] describe a method that extracts the silhouette of a walking figure. They extend the concept by treating changes in shape with a vibration model [24]. They did not report testing their model for recognition.

From a sequence of images, Davis and Bobick [29] compute motion energy images (MEI) and motion-history images (MHI) that indicate where motion is occurring and how recently the motion occurred. They describe the shape of the moving regions with a set of Hu moments, which they in turn use to recognize patterns of motion, such as various aerobic exercises.

Several methods exist to match a kinematic model of a human to a sequence of video images, i.e., estimate a subject's pose. In general, these methods are not gait-specific, nor are they intended to do recognition. They may be viewed as methods for marker-less motion capture. Examples of these methods include work by Hunter et al. [47], Rowley and Rehg [48], Wachter and Nagel [49], Wren et al. [50], Bregler and Malik [51], and Morris and Rehg [52]. One problem with some model-based systems is that they are computationally intensive, which makes them either too slow or too expensive for use in a biometric system.

Bissacco et al. [53] extend results from acquisition of kinematic pose to recognition. They use Bregler's method [54] to extract joint angle trajectories from a motion sequence. They then compute an auto-regressive moving-average (ARMA) model of the joint movement which they in turn use as a feature vector for recognition. Their system can recognize different types of gaits such as running, walking, or walking a staircase. Although they did not test it for biometric gait recognition, this remains as a possibility.

7   Other Applications

Although the subject of this volume is biometrics, we feel it is worth noting some of the other applications that are related to biometric gait analysis.

One area of interest in gait analysis is gait-related pathology. Gait analysis can contribute in two important areas. The first is in diagnosis of gait-related disorders, and the second is in monitoring of treatment. Currently, the norm is to diagnose and monitor treatments using human observations. As in most applications of computer vision, we presume the machine can compensate for human deficiencies. In this case, we expect the machine to give consistent diagnoses and assessments of treatment that do not vary with the individual clinician, their training and experience, or their attentiveness at any particular moment.

Although improvements in human athletic performance are not likely to have an impact on quality of life for most people, athletics do have value as a source of entertainment. To that end, there is interest in evaluating human motion to predict athletic potential, or evaluate training.

Motion capture plays a vital role in the computer graphics and games industry. Currently, marker-based systems dominate industrial motion capture, but advances in human motion analysis are constantly improving marker-less systems. We expect that marker-less systems will eventually become the norm for motion capture.

8   Conclusions

Interest in gait-based biometrics has lead to a stream of recent results. Fig. 8, although not comprehensive, indicates what has been accomplished to date.

Clearly, the performance of gait recognition systems is below what is required for use in biometrics. When one considers that gait is best suited to recognition or surveillance scenarios where the databases are likely to be very large, one would expect high false alarm rates that will render a system useless. Furthermore, tests to date do not fully consider variation in gait measurements over long time spans, and under with different imaging conditions. Nevertheless, researchers are making progress and understanding more about gait with each new development. Areas that need further investigation include studies on variability with terrain, footwear, long time spans, and other confounding factors, in an effort to find gait features that vary only with the individual.

References

[1] McGrath, B.: The week in walks. The New Yorker **June 2** (2003) 35
[2] Johansson, G.: Visual perception of biological motion and a model for its analysis. Perception and Psychophysics **14** (1973) 201–211
[3] Johansson, G.: Visual motion perception. Scientific American (1975) 76–88
[4] Bertenthal, B.I., Pinto, J.: Complementary processes in the perception and production of human movements. In Smith, L.B., Thelen, E., eds.: A Dynamic Systems Approach to Development: Applications. MIT Press, Cambridge, MA (1993) 209–239
[5] Cohen, L., Shipley, T.F., Marshark, E., Taht, K., Aster, D.: Detecting animals in point-light displays. In: Twenty Second Annual Meeting of the Cognitive Science Society, Philadelphia, PA (2000) 70
[6] Bhanu, B., Han, J.: Bayesian-based performance prediction for gait recognition. In: IEEE Workshop on Motion and Video Computing, Orlando, Florida (2002) 145–150
[7] McGeer, T.: Passive dynamic walking. The International Journal of Robotics Research **9** (1990) 62–82
[8] McGeer, T.: Passive walking with knees. In: IEEE International conference on Robotics and Automation. (1990) 1640–1645
[9] Coleman, M.J., Ruina, A.: An uncontrolled toy that can walk but cannot stand still. Physcial Review Letters **80** (1998) 3658–3661
[10] Garcia, M., Chatterjee, A., Ruina, A., Coleman, M.: The simplest walking model: stability, complexity, and scaling. ASME Journal of Biomechanical Engineering **120** (1998) 281–288
[11] Collins, S.H., Wisse, M., Ruina, A.: A 3-d passive-dynamic walking robot with two legs and knees. International Journal of Robotics Research (2001) In Press.
[12] Barclay, C.D., Cutting, J.E., Kozlowski, L.T.: Temporal and spatial factors in gait perception that influence gender recognition. Perception and Psychophysics **23** (1978) 145–152
[13] Kozlowski, L.T., Cutting, J.E.: Recognizing the sex of a walker from a dynamic point-light display. Perception and Psychophysics **21** (1977) 575–580
[14] Cutting, J.E., Kozlowski, L.T.: Recognizing friends by their walk: gait perception without familiarity cues. Bulletin of the Psychonomic Society **9** (1977) 353–356
[15] Laszlo, J., van de Panne, M., Fiume, E.: Limit cycle control and its application to the animation of balancing and walking. In: SIGGRAPH 96. (1996) 155–162
[16] Murray, M.P., Bernard, A., Kory, R.C.: Walking patterns of normal men. The Journal of Bone and Joint Surgery **46A** (1964) 335–359

[17] Murray, M.P.: Gait as a total pattern of movement. American Journal of Physical Medicine **16** (1967) 290–332

[18] von Tscharner, V., Goepfert, B.: Gender dependent emgs of runners resolved by time/frequency and principal pattern analysis. Journal of Electromyography and Kinesiology **13** (2003) 253–272

[19] Sudderth, E., Hunter, E., Kreutz-Delgado, K., Kelly, P.H., Jain, R.: Adaptive video segmentation: theory and real-time implementation. In: 1998 Image Understanding Workshop. Volume 1. (1998) 177–181

[20] Horprasert, T., Harwood, D., Davis, L.: A statistical approach for real time robust background subtraction. In: IEEE Frame Rate Workshop. (1999)

[21] Stauffer, C., Grimson, W.E.L.: Adaptive background mixture models for real-time tracking. In: Computer Vision and Pattern Recognition 99. Volume II. (1999) 246–252

[22] Javed, O., Shafique, K., Shah, M.: A hierarchical approach to robust background subtraction using color and gradient information. In: IEEE Workshop on Motion and Video Computing, Orlando, FL (2002) 22–27

[23] Gross, R., Shi, J.: The cmu motion of body (mobo) database. Technical Report CMU-RI-TR-01-18, Robotics Institute, Carnegie Mellon University (2001)

[24] Baumberg, A.M., Hogg, D.C.: Learning spatiotemporal models from training examples. In: British Machine Vision Conference, Birmingham (1995)

[25] Barron, J.L., Fleet, D.J., Beauchemin, S.S.: Performance of optical flow techniques. International Journal of Computer Vision **12** (1994) 43–77

[26] Horn, B.K.P.: Robot Vision. MIT Press, Cambridge, Massachusetts (1986)

[27] Lucas, B.D., Kanade, T.: An iterative image registration technique with an application to stereo vision. In: International Joint Conference on Artificial Intelligence. (1981) 674–679

[28] Bulthoff, H., Little, J.J., Poggio, T.: A parallel algorithm for real-time computation of optical flow. Nature **337** (1989) 549–553

[29] Davis, J.W., Bobick, A.F.: The representation and recognition of human movement using temporal templates. In: IEEE Computer Vision and Pattern Recognition. (1997) 928–934

[30] Campbell, D.T., Stanley, J.C.: Experimental and Quasi-Experimental Designs for Research. Houghton Mifflin, Boston (1963)

[31] Cohen, P.R.: Empirical Methods for Artificial Intelligence. MIT Press, Cambridge, Massachusetts (1995)

[32] Tanawongsuwan, R., Bobick, A.: Gait recognition from time-normalized joint-angle trajectories in the walking plane. In: Computer Vision and Pattern Recognition 2001. Volume II., Kauai, HI (2001) 726–731

[33] Ben-Abdelkader, C., R.Cutler, Davis, L.: Person identification using automatic height and stride estimation. In: 16th International Conference on Pattern Recognition, Quebec, Quebec (2002) 377–380

[34] Winer, B.J.: Statistical principles in experimental design. McGraw-Hill, New York (1971)

[35] Bobick, A., Johnson, A.: Gait recognitin using static activity-specific parameters. In: Computer Vision and Pattern Recognition 2001. Volume I., Kauai, HI (2001) 423–430

[36] Mardia, K.V., Jupp, P.E.: Directional statistics. Wiley, Chichester (2000)

[37] Little, J.J., Boyd, J.E.: Recognizing people by their gait: the shape of motion. Videre **1** (1998) 1–32

[38] Ben-Abdelkader, C., R.Cutler, Nanda, H., Davis, L.: Eigengait: motion-based recognition of people using image self-similarity. In: Audio- and Video-Based Biometric Person Authentication, Halmstad, Sweden (2001)

[39] Shutler, J.D., Nixon, M.S.: Zernike velocity moments for description and recognition of moving shapes. In: British Machine Vision Conference 2001, Manchester, UK (2001) Session 8: Modelling Behaviour

[40] Cunado, D., NIxon, M.S., Carter, J.N.: Automatic extraction and description of human gait models for recognition purposes. Computer Vision and Image Understanding **90** (2003) 1–41

[41] Boyd, J.E.: Synchronization of oscillations for machine perception of gait. In review (2003)

[42] Boyd, J.E.: Video phase-locked loops in gait recognition. In: International Conference on Computer Vision, Vancouver, BC (2001) 696–703

[43] Kent, J.T.: New directions in shape analysis. In Mardia, K.V., ed.: The art of statistical science: a tribute to g. s. watson. Wiley, Chichester (1992) 115–127

[44] Liu, F., Picard, R.W.: Finding periodicity in space and time. In: International Conference on Computer Vision. (1998)

[45] Polana, R., Nelson, R.: Detection and recognition of periodic, nonrigid motion. International Journal of Computer Vision **23** (1997) 261–282

[46] Baumberg, A.M., Hogg, D.C.: Learning flexible models from image sequences. Technical Report 93.36, University of Leeds School of Computer Studies (1993)

[47] Hunter, E.A., Kelly, P.H., Jain, R.C.: Estimation of articulated motion using kinematically constrained mixture densities. In: Nonrigid and Articulated Motion Workshop, San Juan, Peurto Rico (1997)

[48] Rowley, H.A., Rehg, J.M.: Analyzing articulated motion using expectation-maximization. In: Computer Vision and Pattern Recognition 97, San Juan, Peurto Rico (1997) 935–941

[49] Wachter, S., Nagel, H.H.: Tracking of persons in monocular image sequences. In: Nonrigid and Articulated Motion Workshop, San Juan, Peurto Rico (1997)

[50] Wren, C., Azarbayenjani, A., Darrell, T., Pentland, A.P.: Pfinder: real-time tracking of the human body. IEEE Transactions on Pattern Analysis and Machine Intelligence **19** (1997) 780–785

[51] Bregler, C., Malik, J.: Tracking people with twists and exponential maps. In: Computer Vision and Pattern Recognition 1998, Santa Barbara (1998)

[52] Morris, D.D., Rehg, J.M.: Singularity analysis for articulated object tracking. In: Computer Vision and Pattern Recognition 98, Santa Barbara, CA (1998) 289–296

[53] Bissacco, A., Chiuso, A., Ma, Y., Soatto, S.: Recognition of human gaits. In: Computer Vision and Pattern Recognition 2001. Volume II., Kauai, HI (2001) 52–57

[54] Bregler, C.: Learning and recognizing human dynamics in video sequences. In: Computer Vision and Pattern Recognition 1997, San Juan, Puerto Rico (1997) 568–574

A Tutorial on Fingerprint Recognition[1]

Davide Maltoni

Biometric Systems Laboratory - DEIS - University of Bologna
via Sacchi 3, 47023, Cesena (FC) - Italy
maltoni@csr.unibo.it
http://bias.csr.unibo.it/research/biolab

Abstract. This tutorial introduces fingerprint recognition systems and their main components: sensing, feature extraction and matching. The basic technologies are surveyed and some state-of-the-art algorithms are discussed. Due to the extent of this topic it is not possible to provide here all the details and to cover a number of interesting issues such as classification, indexing and multimodal systems. Interested readers can find in [21] a complete and comprehensive guide to fingerprint recognition.

1 Introduction

A *fingerprint-based biometric system* is essentially a pattern recognition system that recognizes a person by determining the authenticity of her fingerprint. Depending on the application context, a fingerprint-based biometric system may be called either a *verification* system or an *identification* system:

- a verification system authenticates a person's identity by comparing the captured fingerprints with her own biometric template(s) pre-stored in the system. It conducts one-to-one comparison to determine whether the identity claimed by the individual is true;
- an identification system recognizes an individual by searching the entire template database for a match. It conducts one-to-many comparisons to establish the identity of the individual.

Throughout this paper the generic term *recognition* is used where it is not necessary distinguishing between verification and identification.

The block diagrams of a fingerprint-based verification system and an identification system are depicted in Figure 1; user enrollment, which is common to both tasks is also graphically illustrated. The enrollment module is responsible for registering individuals in the biometric system database (system DB). During the enrollment phase, the fingerprint of an individual is acquired by a fingerprint scanner to produce a raw digital representation. A quality check is generally performed to ensure that the acquired sample can be reliably processed by successive stages. In order to facilitate matching, the raw digital representation is usually further processed by a feature ex-

---

[1] Portions reprinted from: D. Maltoni, D. Maio, A.K. Jain and S. Prabhakar, "Handbook of Fingerprint Recognition," Springer, 2003. ©2003 Springer.

M. Tistarelli, J. Bigun, and E. Grosso (Eds.): Biometrics School 2003, LNCS 3161, pp. 43-68, 2005.
© Springer-Verlag Berlin Heidelberg 2005

tractor to generate a compact but expressive representation, called a *template*. The verification task is responsible for verifying individuals at the point of access. During the operation phase, the user's name or PIN (Personal Identification Number) is entered through a keyboard (or a keypad); the biometric reader captures the fingerprint of the individual to be recognized and converts it to a digital format, which is further processed by the feature extractor to produce a compact digital representation. The resulting representation is fed to the feature matcher, which compares it against the template of a single user (retrieved from the system DB based on the user's PIN).

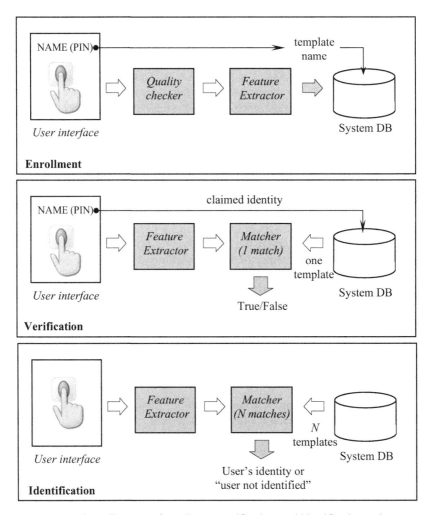

Fig. 1. Block diagrams of enrollment, verification, and identification tasks.

In the identification task, no PIN is provided and the system compares the representation of the input biometric against the templates of all the users in the system database; the output is either the identity of an enrolled user or an alert message such as "user not identified." Because identification in large databases is computationally expensive, classification and indexing techniques are often deployed to limit the number of templates that have to be matched against the input.

It is evident from Figure 1 that the main building blocks of any fingerprint-based verification and identification system are: 1) *sensing*, 2) *feature extraction*, and 3) *matching*. The rest of this paper, after a brief subsection introducing biometric system errors, dedicates a separate section to each of the three above topics.

1.1 Performance of a Fingerprint-Based Recognition System

No biometric system is perfect. Although the accuracy of fingerprint-based biometric systems can be very high (see FVC2002 results [18]), the output is affected by two types of errors: mistaking biometric measurements from two different fingers to be from the same finger (called *false match*) and mistaking two biometric measurements from the same finger to be from two different fingers (called *false non-match*). Note that these two types of errors are also often denoted as *false acceptance* and *false rejection*, but the notation "false match/false non-match" is generally preferable because it is not application dependent [21]. There is a strict tradeoff between FMR (*false match rate*) and FNMR (*false non-match rate*) in every biometric system [8]. In fact, both FMR and FNMR are functions of a system accuracy threshold t. If t is decreased to make the system more tolerant with respect to input variations and noise, then *FMR* increases; vice versa, if t is raised to make the system more secure, then *FNMR* increases accordingly. Besides FMR and FNMR, a "compact" value is generally used to summarize the accuracy of a verification system: the *Equal-Error Rate* (EER) denotes the error rate at the threshold t for which false match rate and false non-match rate are identical: $FMR = FNMR$.

2 Fingerprint Sensing

Historically, in law enforcement applications, the acquisition of fingerprint images was performed by using the so-called "ink-technique": the subject's finger was spread with black ink and pressed against a paper card; the card was then scanned by using a common paper-scanner, producing the final digital image. This kind of process is referred to as *off-line* fingerprint acquisition or off-line sensing. A particular case of off-line sensing is the acquisition of a latent fingerprint from a crime scene. Nowadays, most civil and criminal AFIS accept *live-scan* digital images acquired by directly sensing the finger surface with an electronic fingerprint scanner. No ink is required in this method, and all that a subject has to do is press his finger against the flat surface of a live-scan scanner. To maximize compatibility between digital fingerprint images and ensure good quality of the acquired fingerprint impressions, the US Criminal Justice Information Services released a set of specifications that regulate the quality and format of both fingerprint images and FBI-compliant off-line/live-scan scanners (ref. to Appendix F and Appendix G of CJIS [6]).

2.1 Fingerprint Images

The main parameters characterizing a digital fingerprint image are as follows.

- *Resolution*: This indicates the number of dots or pixels per inch (*dpi*). 500 dpi is the minimum resolution for FBI-compliant scanners and is met by many commercial devices; 250 to 300 dpi is probably the minimum resolution that allows the extraction algorithms to locate the minutiae in fingerprint patterns.

- *Area*: The size of the rectangular area sensed by a fingerprint scanner is a fundamental parameter. The larger the area, the more ridges and valleys are captured and the more distinctive the fingerprint becomes. An area greater than or equal to 1 × 1 square inches (as required by FBI specifications) permits a full plain fingerprint impression to be acquired. In most of the recent fingerprint scanners aimed at non-AFIS market, area is sacrificed to reduce cost and to have a smaller device size. Small-area scanners do not allow a whole fingerprint to be captured, and the users encounter difficulties in re-presenting the same portion of the finger. This may result in a small overlap between different acquisitions of the same finger, leading to false non-match errors.

- *Number of pixels*: The number of pixels in a fingerprint image can be simply derived by the resolution and the fingerprint area: a scanner working at r dpi over an area of $height(h) \times width(w)\ inch^2$ has $rh \times rw$ pixels.

- *Dynamic range (or depth)*: This denotes the number of bits used to encode the intensity value of each pixel. The FBI standard for pixel bit depth is 8 bits, which yields 256 levels of gray.

- *Geometric accuracy*: This is usually specified by the maximum geometric distortion introduced by the acquisition device, and expressed as a percentage with respect to x and y directions.

- *Image quality*: It is not easy to precisely define the quality of a fingerprint image, and it is even more difficult to decouple the fingerprint image quality from the intrinsic finger quality or status. In fact, when the ridge prominence is very low (especially for manual workers and elderly people), when the fingers are too moist or too dry, or when they are incorrectly presented, most of the scanners produce poor quality images (see Figure 2).

2.2 Off-line Acquisition

- Although the first fingerprint scanners were introduced more than 30 years ago, nowadays, the ink-technique [17] is still used in law enforcement applications. Live-scan acquisition techniques are now being employed in AFIS. As a result, the databases built by law enforcement agencies over a period of time contain both the fingerprint images acquired by off-line scanners and live-scan scanners and the AFIS matching algorithms are expected to interoperate on these different types of images.

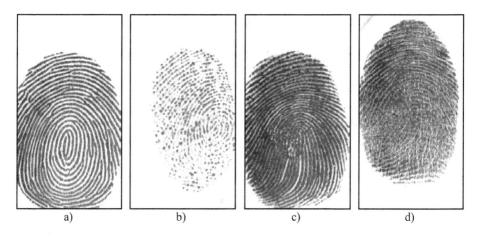

| a) | b) | c) | d) |

Fig. 2. Examples of fingerprint images acquired with an optical scanner: a) a good quality fingerprint; b) a fingerprint left by a dry finger; c) a fingerprint left by a wet finger, d) an intrinsically bad fingerprint.

In the ink-technique the finger skin is first spread with black ink and then pressed against a paper card; the card is then converted into digital form by means of a paper-scanner or by using a high-quality CCD camera (see Figure 3). The default resolution is 500 dpi. If not executed with care, the ink-technique produces images including regions with missing information, due to excessive inkiness or due to ink deficiency. On the other hand, an advantage of this technique is the possibility of producing rolled impressions (by rolling "nail-to-nail" a finger against the card, thus producing an unwrapped representation of the whole pattern) which carries more information with respect to the flat (or dab) impressions obtained by simply pressing the finger against the flat surface of a scanner.

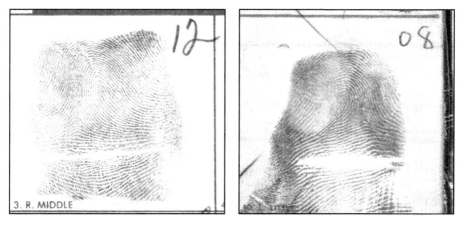

Fig. 3. Rolled fingerprint images acquired off-line with the ink technique.

2.3 Live-Scan Sensing

The most important part of a fingerprint scanner is the sensor (or sensing element), which is the component where the fingerprint image is formed. Almost all the existing sensors belong to one of the three families: optical, solid-state, and ultrasound.

- *Optical sensors.* Frustrated Total Internal Reflection (FTIR) is the oldest and most used live-scan acquisition technique today. The finger touches the top side of a glass prism, but while the ridges enter in contact with the prism surface, the valleys remain at a certain distance (see Figure 4.a); the left side of the prism is illuminated through a diffused light. The light entering the prism is reflected at the valleys, and absorbed at the ridges. The lack of reflection allows the ridges to be discriminated from the valleys. The light rays exit from the right side of the prism and are focused through a lens onto a CCD or CMOS image sensor. In spite of a generally better image quality and the possibility of larger sensing areas, FTIR-based devices cannot be miniaturized unlike other techniques: optical fibers, electro-optical devices, and solid-state devices.

- *Solid-state sensors.* Solid-state sensors (also known as silicon sensors) became commercially available in the middle 1990s. All silicon-based sensors consist of an array of pixels, each pixel being a tiny sensor itself. The user directly touches the surface of the silicon: neither optical components nor external CCD/CMOS image sensors are needed. Four main effects have been proposed to convert the physical information into electrical signals: capacitive, thermal, electric field, and piezoelectric. A capacitive sensor is a two-dimensional array of micro-capacitor plates embedded in a chip (see Figure 4.b). The other plate of each micro-capacitor is the finger skin itself. Small electrical charges are created between the surface of the finger and each of the silicon plates when a finger is placed on the chip. The magnitude of these electrical charges depends on the distance between the fingerprint surface and the capacitance plates.

- *Ultrasound sensors.* Ultrasound sensing may be viewed as a kind of echography. Characteristic of sound waves is the ability to penetrate materials, giving a partial echo at each impedance change. An ultrasound sensor is based on sending acoustic signals toward the fingertip and capturing the echo signal (see Figure 4.c). The echo signal is used to compute the range image of the fingerprint and, subsequently, the ridge structure itself. Good quality images may be obtained by this technology. However, the scanner is large with mechanical parts and quite expensive. Moreover, it takes a few seconds to acquire an image. Hence, this technology is not yet mature enough for large-scale production.

Table 1 lists some commercial scanners designed for the non-AFIS markets, whose cost is less than $200 US. Except for ultrasound scanners, which are not ready for mass-market applications yet, Table 1 includes at least one scanner for each technology. Examples of the same fingerprint (from a good-quality finger, a dry finger, a wet finger, and a poor quality finger, respectively) as acquired by using many of the scanners listed in Table 1 are reported in [21].

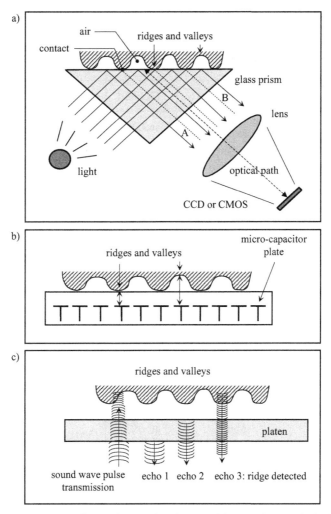

Fig. 4. a) FTIR-based optical fingerprint sensing; b) capacitive sensing; c) the basic principle of the ultrasound technique.

3   Feature Extraction

A fingerprint is the reproduction of a fingertip epidermis, produced when a finger is pressed against a smooth surface. The most evident structural characteristic of a fingerprint is a pattern of interleaved *ridges* and *valleys*; in a fingerprint image, ridges (also called ridge lines) are dark whereas valleys are bright (see Figure 5.a). Ridges and valleys often run in parallel; sometimes they bifurcate and sometimes they terminate.

Table 1. Some commercial scanners, grouped by technology. The table reports for each scanner, the resolution, the sensing area, and the number of pixels.

	Technology	Company	Model	Dpi	Area (h×w)	Pixels
Optical	FTIR	Biometrika www.biometrika.it/eng/	FX2000	569	0.98"×0.52"	560×296 (165,760)
	FTIR	Digital Persona www.digitalpersona.com	UareU2000	440	0.67"×0.47"	316×228 (72,048)
	FTIR (sweep)	Kinetic Sciences www.kinetic.bc.ca	K-1000	up to 1000	0.002"×0.6"	2×900 (H×900)
	FTIR	Secugen www.secugen.com	Hamster	500	0.64"×0.54"	320×268 (85,760)
	Sheet prism	Identix www.identix.com	DFR 200	380	0.67"×0.67"	256×256 (65,535)
	Fiber optic	Delsy www.delsy.com	CMOS module	508	0.71"×0.47"	360×240 (86,400)
	Electro-optical	Ethentica www.ethentica.com	TactilSense T-FPM	403	0.76"×0.56"	306×226 (69,156)
Solid-state	Capacitive (sweep)	Fujitsu www.fme.fujitsu.com	MBF300	500	0.06"×0.51"	32×256 (H×256)
	Capacitive	Infineon www.infineon.com	FingerTip	513	0.56"×0.44"	288×224 (64,512)
	Capacitive	ST-Microelectronics us.st.com	TouchChip TCS1AD	508	0.71"×0.50"	360×256 (92,160)
	Capacitive	Veridicom www.veridicom.com	FPS110	500	0.60"×0.60"	300×300 (90,000)
	Thermal (sweep)	Atmel www.atmel.com	FingerChip AT77C101B	500	0.02"×0.55"	8×280 (H×280)
	Electric field	Authentec www.authentec.com	AES4000	250	0.38"×0.38"	96×96 (9,216)
	Piezoelectric	BMF www.bm-f.com	BLP-100	406	0.92"×"0.63	384×256 (98,304)

When analyzed at the global level, the fingerprint pattern exhibits one or more regions where the ridge lines assume distinctive shapes (characterized by high curvature, frequent termination, etc.). These regions (called *singularities* or *singular regions*) may be classified into three typologies: *loop*, *delta*, and *whorl* (see Figure 5.b). Singular regions belonging to loop, delta, and whorl types are typically characterized by ∩, Δ, and O shapes, respectively. Several fingerprint matching algorithms pre-align fingerprint images according to a landmark or a center point, called the *core*. The core point corresponds to the center of the north most loop type singularity. For fingerprints that do not contain loop or whorl singularities (e.g., those belonging to the Arch class in Figure 6), it is difficult to define the core. In these cases, the core is usually associated with the point of maximum ridge line curvature. Unfortunately, due to the high variability of fingerprint patterns, it is difficult to reliably locate a registration (core) point in all the fingerprint images.

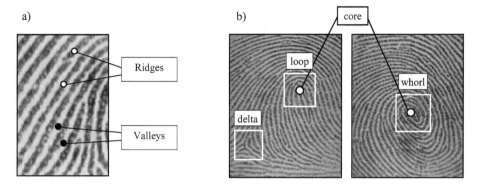

Fig. 5. a) Ridges and valleys on a fingerprint image; b) singular regions (white boxes) and core points (small circles) in fingerprint images.

Singular regions are commonly used for fingerprint classification [21] (see Figure 6), that is, assigning a fingerprint to a class among a set of distinct classes, with the aim of simplifying search and retrieval.

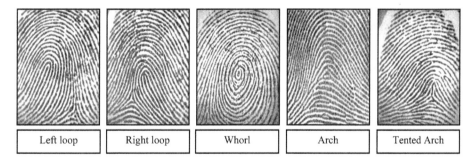

Fig. 6. One fingerprint from each of the five major classes.

At the local level, other important features, called *minutiae* can be found in the fingerprint patterns. Minutia refers to various ways that the ridges can be discontinuous. For example, a ridge can suddenly come to an end (termination), or can divide into two ridges (bifurcation). Although several types of minutiae can be considered, usually only a coarse classification is adopted to deal with the practical difficulty in automatically discerning the different types with high accuracy. The FBI minutiae-coordinate model [25] considers only terminations and bifurcations: each minutia is denoted by its class, the *x*- and *y*-coordinates and the angle between the tangent to the ridge line at the minutia position and the horizontal axis (Figures 7).

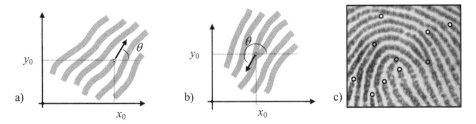

Fig. 7. a) A termination minutia: $[x_0, y_0]$ are the minutia coordinates; θ is the angle that the minutia tangent forms with the horizontal axis; b) a bifurcation minutia: θ is now defined by means of the termination minutia corresponding to the original bifurcation that exists in the negative image; c) termination (white) and bifurcation (gray) minutiae in a sample fingerprint.

Although some fingerprint matching techniques directly compare images through correlation-based methods, the gray-scale image intensities are known to be an unstable representation. Most of the fingerprint recognition and classification algorithms require a feature extraction stage for identifying salient features. The features extracted from fingerprint images often have a direct physical counterpart (e.g., singularities or minutiae), but sometimes they are not directly related to any physical traits (e.g., local orientation image or filter responses). Features may be used either for matching or their computation may serve as an intermediate step for the derivation of other features. For example, some preprocessing and enhancement steps are often performed to simplify the task of minutiae extraction. Figure 9 provides a graphical representation of the main feature extraction steps and their interrelations.

3.1 Local Ridge Orientation and Frequency

The local ridge orientation at $[x,y]$ is the angle θ_{xy} that the fingerprint ridges, crossing through an arbitrary small neighborhood centered at $[x,y]$, form with the horizontal axis (Figure 8).

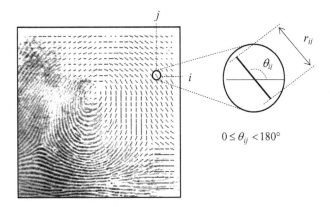

Fig. 8. A fingerprint image faded into the corresponding orientation image computed over a square-meshed grid. Each element denotes the local orientation of the fingerprint ridges; the element length is proportional to its reliability.

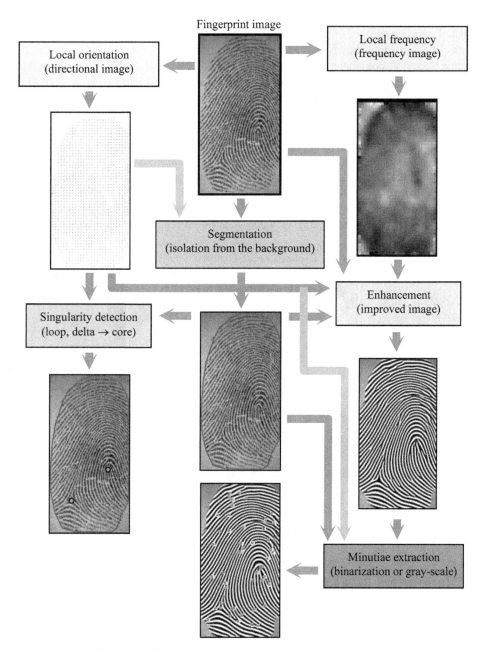

Fig. 9. Graphical representation of fingerprint feature extraction steps and their interrelations. Computation of ridge local orientation and frequency are usually performed at the very beginning since they are useful for most of the other processing steps such as enhancement, singularity detection, segmentation and minutiae extraction.

The simplest and most natural approach for extracting local ridge orientation is based on computation of gradient phase angles. This method, although simple and efficient, has some drawbacks. First, using the classical convolution masks to determine ∇_x and ∇_y components of the gradient, and computing θ_{ij} as the arctangent of the ∇_y/∇_x ratio, presents problems due to the non-linearity and discontinuity around 90°. Second, a single orientation estimate reflects the ridge–valley orientation at too fine a scale and is generally very sensitive to the noise in the fingerprint image.

Robust computation, based on local averaging of gradient estimates, have been proposed by Kass and Witkin [13], Donahue and Rokhlin [7], Ratha, Chen, and Jain [22], and Bazen and Gerez [3].

The local ridge frequency (or density) f_{xy} at point $[x,y]$ is the inverse of the number of ridges per unit length along a hypothetical segment centered at $[x,y]$ and orthogonal to the local ridge orientation θ_{xy}. The local ridge frequency varies across different fingers, and may also noticeably vary across different regions in the same fingerprint (see Figure 10).

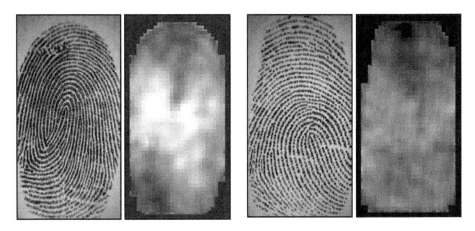

Fig. 10. Two fingerprint images and the corresponding frequency image computed with the method proposed by Maio and Maltoni [20]. Light blocks denote higher frequencies. It is quite evident that significant changes may characterize different fingerprint regions and different average frequencies may result from different fingers.

Hong, Wan, and Jain [10] estimate local ridge frequency by counting the average number of pixels between two consecutive peaks of gray-levels along the direction normal to the local ridge orientation. In the method proposed by Maio and Maltoni [20], the ridge pattern is locally modeled as a sinusoidal-shaped surface, and the variation theorem is exploited to estimate the unknown frequency. Kovacs-Vajna, Rovatti, and Frazzoni [15] proposed a two-step procedure: first, the average ridge distance is estimated in the Fourier domain for each 64×64 sub-block of the image that is of sufficient quality and then this information is propagated, according to a diffusion equation, to the remaining regions.

3.2 Segmentation

Separating the fingerprint area from the background is useful to avoid extraction of features in noisy areas of the fingerprint and background. Because fingerprint images are striated patterns, using a global or local thresholding technique [9] does not allow the fingerprint area to be effectively isolated. In fact, what really discriminates foreground and background is not the average image intensities but the presence of a striped and oriented pattern in the foreground and of an isotropic pattern (i.e., which does not have a dominant orientation) in the background. If the image background were always uniform and lighter than the fingerprint area, a simple approach based on local intensity could be effective for discriminating foreground and background; in practice, the presence of noise (such as that produced by dust and grease on the surface of live-scan fingerprint scanners) requires more robust segmentation techniques [22][19][2].

3.3 Singularity Detection

Most of the approaches proposed in the literature for singularity detection operate on the fingerprint orientation image. The best-known method is based on Poincaré index (Kawagoe and Tojo [14]).

Let C be a closed path defined as an ordered sequence of some elements of the fingerprint orientation image[2] such that $[i,j]$ is an internal point (see Figure 11), then the Poincaré index $P_{G,C}(i,j)$ at $[i,j]$ is computed by algebraically summing the orientation differences between adjacent elements of C. Summing orientation differences requires a direction (among the two possible) to be associated at each orientation. A solution to this problem is to randomly select the direction of the first element and assign the direction closest to that of the previous element to each successive element.

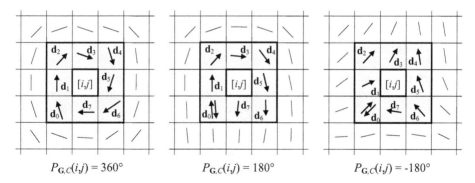

$$P_{G,C}(i,j) = 360° \qquad P_{G,C}(i,j) = 180° \qquad P_{G,C}(i,j) = -180°$$

Fig. 11. Examples of computation of the Poincaré index in the 8-neighborhood of points belonging (from the left to the right) to a whorl, loop, and delta singularity, respectively.

---

[2] The fingerprint orientation image is a matrix whose elements encode the local orientation of the fingerprint ridges.

It is well known and can be easily shown that, on closed curves, the Poincaré index assumes only one of the discrete values: $0°$, $\pm180°$, and $\pm360°$. In the case of fingerprint singularities:

$$P_{G,C}(i,j) = \begin{cases} 0° & \text{if } [i,j] \text{ does not belong to any singular region} \\ 360° & \text{if } [i,j] \text{ belongs to a whorl type singular region} \\ 180° & \text{if } [i,j] \text{ belongs to a loop type singular region} \\ -180° & \text{if } [i,j] \text{ belongs to a delta type singular region.} \end{cases}$$

An example of singularities detected by the above method is shown in Figure 12.

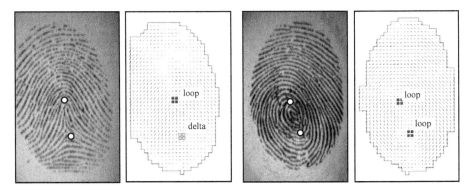

Fig. 12. Singularity detection by using the Poincaré index method. The elements whose Poincaré index is $180°$ (loop) or $-180°$ (delta) are enclosed by small boxes.

A number of alternative approaches have been proposed for singularity detection; they can be coarsely classified in: 1) methods based on local characteristics of the orientation image, 2) partitioning-based methods, 3) core detection and fingerprint registration approaches. For further details refer to [21].

3.4 Enhancement and Binarization

The performance of minutiae extraction algorithms and other fingerprint recognition techniques relies heavily on the quality of the input fingerprint images. In an ideal fingerprint image, ridges and valleys alternate and flow in a locally constant direction. In such situations, the ridges can be easily detected and minutiae can be precisely located in the image. However, in practice, due to skin conditions (e.g., wet or dry, cuts, and bruises), sensor noise, incorrect finger pressure, and inherently low-quality fingers (e.g., elderly people, manual workers), a significant percentage of fingerprint images (approximately 10%) is of poor quality like those in Figures 2.b, c and d.

The goal of an enhancement algorithm is to improve the clarity of the ridge structures in the recoverable regions and mark the unrecoverable regions as too noisy for further processing. Usually, the input of the enhancement algorithm is a gray-scale image. The output may either be a gray-scale or a binary image, depending on the algorithm.

General-purpose image enhancement techniques do not produce satisfying and definitive results for fingerprint image enhancement. The most widely used technique for fingerprint image enhancement is based on *contextual filters*. In conventional image filtering, only a single filter is used for convolution throughout the image. In contextual filtering, the filter characteristics change according to the local context. Usually, a set of filters is pre-computed and one of them is selected for each image region. In fingerprint enhancement, the context is often defined by the local ridge orientation and local ridge frequency. In fact, the sinusoidal-shaped wave of ridges and valleys is mainly defined by a local orientation and frequency that varies slowly across the fingerprint area. An appropriate filter that is tuned to the local ridge frequency and orientation can efficiently remove the undesired noise and preserve the true ridge and valley structure.

Hong, Wan, and Jain [10] proposed an effective method based on Gabor filters. Gabor filters have both frequency-selective and orientation-selective properties and have optimal joint resolution in both spatial and frequency domains. A graphical representation of a bank of 24 filters and an example of their applications is shown in Figure 13. Further information on the huge number of existing fingerprint enhancement and binarization techniques can be found in [21].

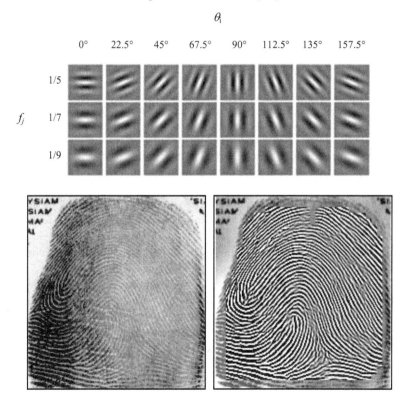

Fig. 13. A graphical representation of a bank of 24 Gabor filters and their application to the enhancement of a noisy image.

3.5 Minutiae Extraction

Although rather different from one another, most of the proposed methods require the fingerprint gray-scale image to be converted into a binary image. Some binarization processes greatly benefit from an a priori enhancement; on the other hand, some enhancement algorithms directly produce a binary output, and therefore the distinction between enhancement and binarization is often faded. The binary images obtained by the binarization process are usually submitted to a thinning stage [16] which allows for the ridge line thickness to be reduced to one pixel. Finally, a simple image scan allows the detection of pixels that correspond to minutiae through the pixel-wise computation of crossing number[3] (see Figure 14).

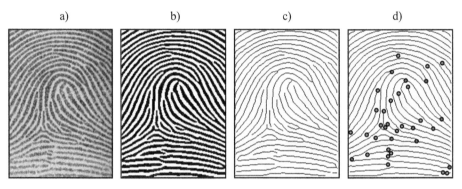

Fig. 14. a) A fingerprint gray-scale image; b) the image obtained after enhancement and binarization; c) the image obtained after thinning; d) termination and bifurcation minutiae detected through the pixel-wise computation of the crossing number.

Some authors have proposed minutiae extraction approaches that work directly on the gray-scale images without binarization and thinning. This choice is motivated by these considerations:

- a significant amount of information may be lost during the binarization process;
- binarization and thinning are time consuming; thinning may introduce a large number of spurious minutiae;
- in the absence of an a priori enhancement step, most of the binarization techniques do not provide satisfactory results when applied to low-quality images.

Maio and Maltoni [19] proposed a direct gray-scale minutiae extraction technique, whose basic idea is to track the ridge lines in the gray-scale image, by "sailing" according to the local orientation of the ridge pattern. The ridge line extraction algorithm attempts to locate, at each step, a local maximum relative to a section orthogonal to the ridge direction. By connecting the consecutive maxima, a polygonal ap-

---

[3] The crossing number of a pixel in a binary image is defined as half the sum of the differences between pairs of adjacent pixels in the 8-neighborhood [21]; its value is 1 for a termination minutia, 2 for an intermediate ridge pixel, and ≥ 3 for a bifurcation or a more complex minutia.

proximation of the ridge line can be obtained. See Figure 15 for an example of direct gray-scale minutiae extraction.

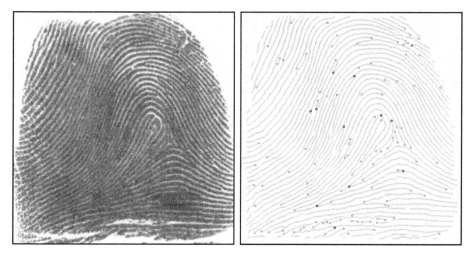

Fig. 15. Minutiae detection on a sample fingerprint by using the Maio and Maltoni [19] method.

A post-processing stage (called *minutiae filtering*) is often useful in removing the spurious minutiae detected in highly corrupted regions or introduced by previous processing steps (e.g., thinning). Two main post-processing types have been proposed: structural post-processing, and minutiae filtering in the gray-scale domain [21].

4   Matching

Matching high quality fingerprints with small intra-class variations is not difficult and every reasonable algorithm can do it. The real challenge is matching samples (sometimes very poor quality) affected by:

- *High displacement and/or rotation*: finger displacement and rotation often cause part of the fingerprint area to fall outside the sensor's "field of view," resulting in a smaller overlap between the template and the input fingerprints. This problem is particularly serious for small-area sensors. A finger displacement of just 2 mm (imperceptible to the user) results in a translation of about 40 pixels in a fingerprint image scanned at 500 dpi.
- *Non-linear distortion*: the act of sensing maps the three-dimensional shape of a finger onto the two-dimensional surface of the sensor. This results in a non-linear distortion in successive acquisitions of the same finger due to skin plasticity.
- *Different pressure and skin condition*: the ridge structure of a finger would be accurately captured if ridges of the part of the finger being imaged were in uniform contact with the sensor surface. However, finger pressure, dryness of the

skin, skin disease, sweat, dirt, grease, and humidity in the air all confound the situation, resulting in a non-uniform contact.
- *Feature extraction errors*: the feature extraction algorithms are imperfect and often introduce measurement errors. For example in low-quality fingerprint images, the minutiae extraction process may introduce a large number of spurious minutiae and may not be able to detect all the true minutiae.

The pairs of images in Figure 16.a visually show the high variability (large *intra-class* variations) that can characterize two different impressions of the same finger. On the other hand, as evident from Figure 16.b, fingerprint images from different fingers may sometimes appear quite similar (small *inter-class* variations), especially in terms of global structure (position of the singularities, local ridge orientation, etc.).

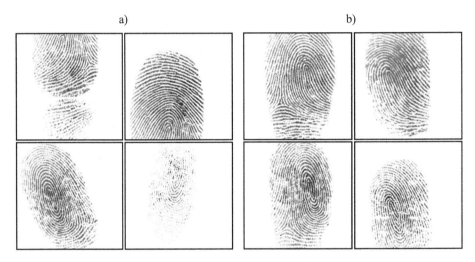

Fig. 16. a) each row shows a pair of impressions of the same finger, taken from the FVC2002 DB1, which were falsely non-matched by most of the algorithms submitted to FVC2002 [18]. The main cause of difficulty is a very small overlap in the first row, and very different skin conditions in the second row; b) each row shows a pair of impressions of different fingers, taken from the FVC2002 databases which were falsely matched by some of the algorithms submitted to FVC2002.

The large number of existing approaches to fingerprint matching can be coarsely classified into three families.
- *Correlation-based matching*: two fingerprint images are superimposed and the correlation between corresponding pixels is computed for different alignments (e.g., various displacements and rotations).
- *Minutiae-based matching*: minutiae are extracted from the two fingerprints and stored as sets of points in the two-dimensional plane. Minutiae-based matching essentially consists of finding the alignment between the template and the input minutiae sets that results in the maximum number of minutiae pairings.
- *Ridge feature-based matching*: the approaches belonging to this family compare fingerprints in term of features extracted from the ridge pattern.

In the rest of this section the representation of the fingerprint acquired during enrollment is denoted to as the *template* (**T**) and the representation of the fingerprint to be matched as the *input* (**I**). In case no feature extraction is performed, the fingerprint representation coincides with the grayscale fingerprint image itself.

4.1 Correlation-Based Techniques

Let $\mathbf{I}^{(\Delta x, \Delta y, \theta)}$ represent a rotation of the input image **I** by an angle θ around the origin (usually the image center) and shifted by Δx, Δy pixels in directions x and y, respectively; then the similarity between the two fingerprint images **T** and **I** can be measured as

$$S(\mathbf{T},\mathbf{I}) = \max_{\Delta x, \Delta y, \theta} CC\left(\mathbf{T},\mathbf{I}^{(\Delta x, \Delta y, \theta)}\right). \tag{1}$$

where $CC(\mathbf{T},\mathbf{I}) = \mathbf{T}^T\mathbf{I}$ is the cross-correlation between **T** and **I**. The cross-correlation [9] is well known measure of image similarity and the maximization in (1) allows to find the optimal registration.

Anyway, the direct application of Equation (1) rarely leads to acceptable results mainly due to the following problems.

- Non-linear distortion makes impressions of the same finger significantly different in terms of global structure; in particular, the elastic distortion does not significantly alter the fingerprint pattern locally, but since the effects of distortion get integrated in image space, two global fingerprint patterns cannot be reliably correlated. The use of local or block-wise correlation techniques can help to deal with this problem [4].
- Skin condition and finger pressure cause image brightness, contrast, and ridge thickness to vary significantly across different impressions. The use of more sophisticated correlation measures may compensate for contrast and brightness variations and applying a proper combination of enhancement, binarization, and thinning steps (performed on both **T** and **I**) may limit the ridge thickness problem.
- A direct application of Equation (1) is computationally very expensive. For example, consider two 400×400 pixel images: if Δx, Δy were both sampled with a one-pixel step in the range $[-200,200]$, and θ with step $1°$ in the range $[-30°,30°]$ it would be necessary to compute $401 \times 401 \times 61$ cross-correlations, resulting in about 1569 billion multiplications and summations (i.e., more than one hour on a 500 MIPS computer). Local correlation and correlation in the Fourier domain can improve efficiency.

4.2 Minutiae-Based Methods

This is the most popular and widely used technique, being the basis of the fingerprint comparison made by fingerprint examiners. Minutiae are extracted from the two fingerprints and stored as sets of points in the two-dimensional plane. Most common minutiae matching algorithms consider each minutia as a triplet $\mathbf{m} = \{x, y, \theta\}$ that indicates the x, y minutia location coordinates and the minutia angle θ:

$$\mathbf{T} = \{\mathbf{m}_1, \mathbf{m}_2, ..., \mathbf{m}_m\}, \quad \mathbf{m}_i = \{x_i, y_i, \theta_i\}, \quad i = 1..m$$
$$\mathbf{I} = \{\mathbf{m}'_1, \mathbf{m}'_2, ..., \mathbf{m}'_n\}, \quad \mathbf{m}'_j = \{x'_j, y'_j, \theta'_j\} \quad j = 1..n,$$

where m and n denote the number of minutiae in $\mathbf{T}$ and $\mathbf{I}$, respectively.

A minutia $\mathbf{m}'_j$ in $\mathbf{I}$ and a minutia $\mathbf{m}_i$ in $\mathbf{T}$ are considered "matching," if the *spatial distance* (*sd*) between them is smaller than a given tolerance r_0 and the *direction difference* (*dd*) between them is smaller than an angular tolerance θ_0:

$$sd(\mathbf{m}'_j, \mathbf{m}_i) = \sqrt{(x'_j - x_i)^2 + (y'_j - y_i)^2} \leq r_0, \qquad \text{and} \qquad (2)$$

$$dd(\mathbf{m}'_j, \mathbf{m}_i) = \min\left(\left|\theta'_j - \theta_i\right|, 360° - \left|\theta'_j - \theta_i\right|\right) \leq \theta_0. \qquad (3)$$

The *tolerance boxes* (or hyper-spheres) defined by r_0 and θ_0 are necessary to compensate for the unavoidable errors made by feature extraction algorithms and to account for the small plastic distortions that cause the minutiae positions to change.

Aligning the two fingerprints is a mandatory step in order to maximize the number of matching minutiae. Correctly aligning two fingerprints certainly requires *displacement* (in x and y) and *rotation* (θ) to be recovered, and likely involves other geometrical transformations like *scale* and specific *distortion-tolerant* geometrical transformations. Let *map*(.) be the function that maps a minutia $\mathbf{m}'_j$ (from $\mathbf{I}$) into $\mathbf{m}''_j$ according to a given geometrical transformation; for example, by considering a displacement of $[\Delta x, \Delta y]$ and a counterclockwise rotation θ around the origin[4]:

$$map_{\Delta x, \Delta y, \theta}(\mathbf{m}'_j = \{x'_j, y'_j, \theta'_j\}) = \mathbf{m}''_j = \{x''_j, y''_j, \theta'_j + \theta\}, \quad \text{where}$$

$$\begin{bmatrix} x''_j \\ y''_j \end{bmatrix} = \begin{bmatrix} \cos\theta & -\sin\theta \\ \sin\theta & \cos\theta \end{bmatrix} \begin{bmatrix} x'_j \\ y'_j \end{bmatrix} + \begin{bmatrix} \Delta x \\ \Delta y \end{bmatrix}.$$

Let *mm*(.) be an indicator function that returns 1 in the case where the minutiae $\mathbf{m}''_j$ and $\mathbf{m}_i$ match according to Equations (2) and (3):

$$mm(\mathbf{m}''_j, \mathbf{m}_i) = \begin{cases} 1 & sd(\mathbf{m}''_j, \mathbf{m}_i) \leq r_0 \quad \text{and} \quad dd(\mathbf{m}''_j, \mathbf{m}_i) \leq \theta_0 \\ 0 & \text{otherwise.} \end{cases}$$

Then, the matching problem can be formulated as

$$\underset{\Delta x, \Delta y, \theta, P}{\text{maximize}} \sum_{i=1}^{m} mm(map_{\Delta x, \Delta y, \theta}(\mathbf{m}'_{P(i)}), \mathbf{m}_i), \qquad (4)$$

where $P(i)$ is an unknown function that determines the *pairing* between $\mathbf{I}$ and $\mathbf{T}$ minutiae; in particular, each minutia has either exactly one mate in the other fingerprint or has no mate at all:

---

4 The origin is usually selected as the minutiae centroid (i.e., the average point).

1. $P(i) = j$ indicates that the mate of the $\mathbf{m}_i$ in $\mathbf{T}$ is the minutia $\mathbf{m}'_j$ in $\mathbf{I}$;
2. $P(i) =$ null indicates that minutia $\mathbf{m}_i$ in $\mathbf{T}$ has no mate in $\mathbf{I}$;
3. a minutia $\mathbf{m}'_j$ in $\mathbf{I}$, such that $\forall\ i = 1..m, P(i) \neq j$ has no mate in $\mathbf{T}$;
4. $\forall\ i = 1..m,\ k = 1..m,\ i \neq k \Rightarrow P(i) \neq P(k)$ or $P(i) = P(k) =$ null (this requires that each minutia in $\mathbf{I}$ is associated with a maximum of one minutia in $\mathbf{T}$).

Note that, in general, $P(i) = j$ does not necessarily mean that minutiae $\mathbf{m}'_j$ and $\mathbf{m}_i$ match in the sense of Equations (2) and (3) but only that they are the most likely pair under the current transformation.

Solving the minutiae matching problem (expression (4)) is trivial if the correct alignment (Δx, Δy, θ) or the function P (minutiae correspondence) is known. Unfortunately, in practice, neither the alignment parameters nor the correspondence function P are known and, therefore, solving the matching problem is very hard. In the pattern recognition literature the minutiae matching problem has been generally addressed as a *point pattern matching* problem [21]. Hough transform-based approaches are the most commonly used techniques for global minutiae matching [23] [5]; an example is shown in Figure 17. The Hough transform techniques [1] converts point pattern matching to the problem of detecting peaks in the Hough space of transformation parameters. It discretizes the parameter space (Δx, Δy, θ) and accumulates evidence in the discretized space by deriving transformation parameters that relate two sets of points using a substructure of the feature matching technique.

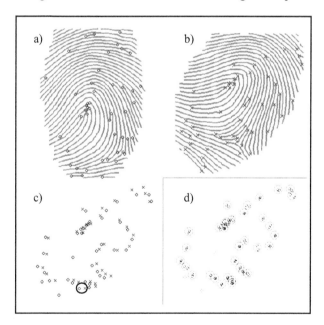

Fig. 17. Minutiae matching by the Chang et al. approach [5]. Figures a) and b) show the minutiae extracted from the template and the input fingerprint, respectively; c) the minutiae are coarsely superimposed and the principal pair is marked with an ellipse; d) each circle denotes a pair of minutiae as mated by the algorithm.

Equation 4 attempts to solve the minutiae matching problem globally (*global minutiae matching*). Some authors proposed "*local minutiae matching*" techniques that consists of comparing two fingerprints according to local minutiae structures (Jiang and Yau [12], Ratha et al. [24]); local structures are characterized by attributes that are invariant with respect to global transformation (e.g., translation, rotation, etc.) and therefore are suitable for matching without any a priori global alignment. Matching fingerprints based only on local minutiae arrangements relaxes global spatial relationships which are highly distinctive and therefore reduce the amount of information available for discriminating fingerprints. Global versus local matching is a tradeoff among simplicity, low computational complexity, and high distortion-tolerance (local matching), and high distinctiveness on the other hand (global matching).

In [12] local structures are formed by a central minutia and its two nearest-neighbor minutiae; the feature vector $\mathbf{v}_i$ associated with the minutia $\mathbf{m}_i$, whose nearest neighbors are minutiae $\mathbf{m}_j$ (the closest to $\mathbf{m}_i$) and $\mathbf{m}_k$ (the second closest) is $\mathbf{v}_i = [d_{ij}, d_{ik}, \theta_{ij}, \theta_{ik}, \varphi_{ij}, \varphi_{ik}, n_{ij}, n_{ik}, t_i, t_j, t_k]$, where d_{ab} is the distance between minutiae $\mathbf{m}_a$ and $\mathbf{m}_b$, θ_{ab} is the direction difference between the angles θ_a and θ_b of $\mathbf{m}_a$ and $\mathbf{m}_b$, φ_{ab} is the direction difference between the angle θ_a of $\mathbf{m}_a$ and the direction of the edge connecting $\mathbf{m}_a$ to $\mathbf{m}_b$, n_{ab} is the ridge count between $\mathbf{m}_a$ and $\mathbf{m}_b$, and t_a is the minutia type of $\mathbf{m}_a$ (Figure 18).

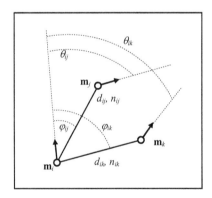

Fig. 18. Features of the local structures used by Jiang and Yau [12].

Local minutiae matching is performed by computing, for each pair of minutiae $\mathbf{m}_i$ and $\mathbf{m}'_j$, $i = 1..m$, $j = 1..n$, a weighted distance between their vectors $\mathbf{v}_i$ and $\mathbf{v}'_j$.

The best matching pair is then selected and used for registering the two fingerprints. In the second stage (consolidation), the feature vectors of the remaining aligned pairs are matched and a final score is computed by taking into account the different contributions (first stage and second stage).

4.3   Ridge Feature-Based Techniques

Three main reasons induce designers of fingerprint recognition techniques to search for other fingerprint distinguishing features, beyond minutiae: 1) reliably extracting minutiae from poor quality fingerprints is very difficult; 2) minutiae extraction is time consuming; 3) additional features may be used in conjunction with minutiae (and not as an alternative) to increase system accuracy and robustness. The more commonly used alternative features are:

1. size of the fingerprint and shape of the external fingerprint silhouette;
2. number, type, and position of singularities;
3. spatial relationship and geometrical attributes of the ridge lines;
4. shape features;
5. global and local texture information;
6. sweat pores;
7. fractal features.

Jain et al. [11] proposed a local texture analysis technique where the fingerprint area of interest is tessellated with respect to the core point (see Figure 19).

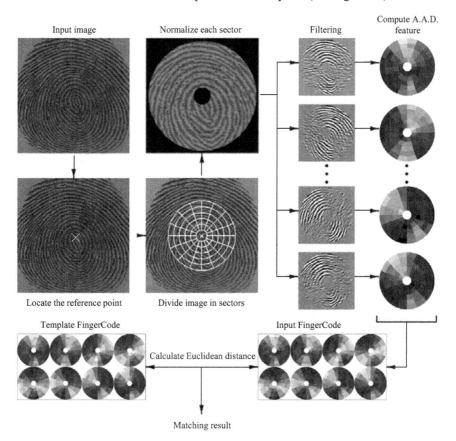

Fig. 19. System diagram of Jain et al.'s FingerCode approach [11].

A feature vector is composed of an ordered enumeration of the features extracted from the local information contained in each sector specified by the tessellation. Thus the feature elements capture the local texture information and the ordered enumeration of the tessellation captures the global relationship among the local contributions. The local texture information in each sector is decomposed into separate channels by using a Gabor filterbank. Each fingerprint is represented by a $80 \times 8 = 640$ fixed-size feature vector, called the *FingerCode*. The generic element V_{ij} of the vector ($i = 1..80$ is the cell index, $j = 1..8$ is the filter index) denotes the energy revealed by the filter j in cell i, and is computed as the average absolute deviation (AAD) from the mean of the responses of the filter j over all the pixels of the cell i. Matching two fingerprints is then translated into matching their respective FingerCodes, which is simply performed by computing the Euclidean distance between two FingerCodes.

5 Conclusions

Recent developments in fingerprint scanners have focused on reducing both their cost and size. Although lower cost and size are essential to enable a wide deployment of the technology in civilian applications, some of these developments have been made at the expense of fingerprint image quality (e.g., dpi resolution, etc.). It is very likely that while the market will continue to drive down scanner prices, it will also require higher-quality products at the same time. Manufacturers will continue to innovate low-cost small-size scanner designs, but they will also take care that their products deliver high quality-images of large areas of the finger.

Robust extraction of fingerprint feature remains a challenging problem, especially in poor quality fingerprints. Development of fingerprint-specific image processing techniques is necessary in order to solve some of the outstanding problems. For example, explicitly measuring (and restoring or masking) noise such as creases, cuts, dryness, smudginess, and the like will be helpful in reducing feature extraction errors. Algorithms that can extract discriminative non-minutiae-based features in fingerprint images and integrate them with the available features and matching strategies will improve fingerprint matching accuracy. New (perhaps, model-based) methods for computation (or restoration) of the orientation image in very low-quality images is also desirable to reduce feature extraction errors.

Most of the fingerprint matching approaches introduced in the last four decades are minutiae-based, but recently correlation-based techniques are receiving renewed interest. New texture-based methods have been proposed and the integration of approaches relying on different features seems to be the most promising way to significantly improve the accuracy of fingerprint recognition systems.

References

1. Ballard, D.H.: Generalizing the Hough Transform to Detect Arbitrary Shapes. Pattern Recognition, vol. 3, no. 2 (1981) 110–122.

2. Bazen, A.M., Gerez, S.H.: Segmentation of Fingerprint Images. Proc. Workshop on Circuits Systems and Signal Processing (ProRISC 2001) (2001) 276–280.

3. Bazen, A.M., Gerez, S.H.: Systematic Methods for the Computation of the Directional Fields and Singular Points of Fingerprints. IEEE Transactions on Pattern Analysis and Machine Intelligence, vol. 24, no. 7 (2002) 905–919.

4. Bazen, A.M., Verwaaijen, G.T.B., Gerez, S.H., Veelenturf, L.P.J., van der Zwaag, B.J.: A Correlation-Based Fingerprint Verification System. Proc. Workshop on Circuits Systems and Signal Processing (ProRISC 2000) (2000) 205–213.

5. Chang, S.H., Cheng, F.H., Hsu, W.H., and Wu, G.Z.: Fast Algorithm for Point Pattern-Matching: Invariant to Translations, Rotations and Scale Changes. Pattern Recognition, vol. 30, no. 2 (1997) 311–320.

6. Criminal Justice Information Services: Electronic Fingerprint Transmission Specification. Int. Report. CJIS-RS-0010 (V7), (1999), available at: http://www.fbi.gov/hq/cjisd/iafis/efts70/cover.htm.

7. Donahue, M.L, Rokhlin, S.I.: On the use of Level Curves in Image Analysis. CVGIP: Image Understanding, vol. 57, no. 2 (1993) 185–203.

8. Golfarelli, M., Maio, D., Maltoni, D.: On the Error-Reject Tradeoff in Biometric Verification Systems. IEEE Transactions on Pattern Analysis and Machine Intelligence, vol. 19, no.7, (1997) 786–796.

9. Gonzales, R.C., Woods, R.E.: Digital Image Processing. Addison-Wesley, Reading, MA (1992).

10. Hong, L., Wan, Y., Jain, A.K.: Fingerprint Image Enhancement: Algorithms and Performance Evaluation. IEEE Transactions on Pattern Analysis and Machine Intelligence, vol. 20, no. 8 (1998) 777–789.

11. Jain, A.K., Prabhakar, S., Hong, L., Pankanti, S.: Filterbank-Based Fingerprint Matching. IEEE Transactions on Image Processing, vol. 9 (2000) 846–859.

12. Jiang, X., Yau, W.Y.: Fingerprint Minutiae Matching Based on the Local and Global Structures. Proc. Int. Conf. on Pattern Recognition (15th), vol. 2 (2000) 1042-1045.

13. Kass, M., Witkin, A.: Analyzing Oriented Patterns. Computer Vision, Graphics, and Image Processing, vol. 37, no. 3 (1987) 362–385.

14. Kawagoe, M., Tojo, A.: Fingerprint Pattern Classification. Pattern Recognition, vol. 17, (1984) 295–303.

15. Kovacs-Vajna, Z.M., Rovatti, R., Frazzoni, M.: Fingerprint Ridge Distance Computation Methodologies. Pattern Recognition, vol. 33, no. 1 (2000) 69–80.

16. Lam, L., Lee, S.W., Suen, C.Y.: Thinning Methodologies: A Comprehensive Survey. IEEE Transactions on Pattern Analysis and Machine Intelligence, vol. 14, no. 9 (1992) 869–885.

17. Lee, H.C., Gaensslen, R.E.: Advances in Fingerprint Technology. 2nd edition, Elsevier, New York (2001).

18. Maio, D., Maltoni, D., Cappelli, R., Wayman, J.L., Jain A.K.: FVC2002: Second Fingerprint Verification Competition. Proc. Int. Conf. on Pattern Recognition (16th), vol. 3 (2002) 811–814.

19. Maio, D., Maltoni, D.: Direct Gray-Scale Minutiae Detection in Fingerprints. IEEE Transactions on Pattern Analysis and Machine Intelligence, vol. 19, no. 1 (1997).

20. Maio, D., Maltoni, D.: Ridge-Line Density Estimation in Digital Images. Proc. Int. Conf. on Pattern Recognition (14th) (1998) 534–538.

21. Maltoni, D., Maio, D., Jain, A.K., Prabhakar, S.: Handbook of Fingerprint Recognition, Springer, New York (2003).

22. Ratha, N.K., Chen, S.Y., Jain, A.K.: Adaptive Flow Orientation-Based Feature Extraction in Fingerprint Images. Pattern Recognition, vol. 28, no. 11 (1995) 1657–1672.

23. Ratha, N.K., Karu, K., Chen, S., Jain, A.K.: A Real-Time Matching System for Large Fingerprint Databases. IEEE Transactions on Pattern Analysis and Machine Intelligence, vol. 18, no. 8 (1996) 799–813.

24. Ratha, N.K., Pandit, V.D., Bolle, R.M., Vaish, V.: Robust Fingerprint Authentication Using Local Structural Similarity. Proc. Workshop on Applications of Computer Vision (2000) 29–34.

25. Wegstein, J.H.: An Automated Fingerprint Identification System. U.S. Government Publication, Washington, DC: U.S. Dept. of Commerce, National Bureau of Standards (1982).

Spiral Topologies for Biometric Recognition

Massimo Tistarelli[1], Enrico Grosso[1], Andrea Lagorio[2]

[1] University of Sassari
Computer Vision Laboratory
piazza Duomo, 6 – 07041 Alghero (SS) - Italy
tista, grosso@uniss.it
http://www.uniss.it

[2] DIST - University of Genova
Computer Vision Laboratory
via Opera Pia, 13 – 16145 Genova - Italy
lemmings@dist.unige.it
http://www.dist.unige.it

Abstract. Biometric recognition has attracted the attention of scientists, investors, government agencies as well as the media for the great potential in many application domains. It turns out that there are still a number of intrinsic drawbacks in all biometric techniques. In this paper we postulate the need for a proper data representation which may simplify and augment the discrimination among different instances or biometric samples of different subjects. Considering the design of many natural systems it turns out that spiral (circular) topologies are the best suited to economically store and process data. Among the many developed techniques for biometric recognition, face analysis seems to be the most promising and interesting modality. The ability of the human visual system of analyzing unknown faces, is an example of the amount of information which can be extracted from face images. Nonetheless, there are still many open problems which need to be "faced" as well. The choice of optimal resolution of the face within the image, face registration and facial feature extraction are still open issues. This not only requires to devise new algorithms but to determine the real potential and limitations of existing techniques. In this paper two different methods for face matching are presented, based on the same similarity measure but on different image representations. The methods are tested with conventional and also new databases, obtained from real subjects in real working environments.

1 Introduction

Every living creature depends on the ability to perceive the outside world. In turn, the correct perception requires to consistently organize the acquired sensory data, either visual, tactile, olfactory etc. Organized "perceptual patterns" allow humans to perform a variety of tasks, all based on the recognition of precise data configurations.

For example, the first and primary perceptual task of a living creature is the recognition of his/her mother. This is firstly based on simple recording and matching

M. Tistarelli, J. Bigun, and E. Grosso (Eds.): Biometrics School 2003, LNCS 3161, pp. 69-90, 2005.
© Springer-Verlag Berlin Heidelberg 2005

of olfactory data, but quickly develops adding information based on her voice and view. In the case of humans, as the child grows, quickly develops a surprising ability to analyze faces. The neural plasticity of infants allows to generalize the "mom recognition" task to learn how to recognize many different faces.

Not only this, in fact, face analysis in humans is not limited to identity verification: this is Jack and this is Tom. There is a considerable number of inference processes, based on face image analysis, devoted to understand other aspects of the person in front. For example, the age, race, mood, and many other "signals" which may be given and perceived by particular motions of the eyes and the face mussels.

Reverting this human capability into the design of an information technology system is certainly a formidable task. Current research in face recognition and also gesture recognition is trying to "climb the hill" toward this direction [1-14].

Many difficulties arise from the enormous dimensionality of the search space when dealing with natural images (both for the number of elements in a typical data set and for the number of samples for each data element). These findings enforce the need to devise simple and modular processing elements, which are functionally related to the selective extraction of collective information from face image streams.

2   Neurophysiological Evidence

Neural systems that mediate face recognition appear to exist very early in life. In normal infancy, the face holds particular significance and provides nonverbal information important for communication and survival [15]. Face recognition ability is present during the first 6 months of life, while a visual preference for faces and the capacity for very rapid face recognition are present at birth [16,17]. By 4 months, infants recognize upright faces better than upside down faces, and at 6 months, infants show differential event-related brain potentials to familiar versus unfamiliar faces [18,19].

Much is known about the neural systems that subserve face recognition in adult humans and primates.

In the monkey brain over 30 functional areas have been defined clearly devoted to visual information processing. Face-selective neurons have been found in the inferior temporal areas (TEa and TEm), the superior temporal sensory area, the amygdala, the ventral striatum (which receives input from the amygdala) and the inferior convexity [20].

Using functional magnetic resonance imaging (fMRI), an area in the fusiform gyrus was found significantly activated when the subjects viewed faces [21-23]. Within this "general face activation area" specific regions of interest have been reported responding significantly more strongly to passive viewing of:

o   intact than scrambled two-tone faces;

o   full front-view face photos than front-view photos of houses, and three-quarter-view face photos (with hair concealed) than photos of human hands;

Fig. 1. Examples of spiral, space-variant, topologies in the spatial distribution of elements in natural systems.

o   a region also responded more strongly during a consecutive matching task performed on three-quarter-view faces versus hands.

The reported data allowed to reject alternative accounts of the function of the fusiform face area (area "FF") that appeal to visual attention, subordinate-level classification, or general processing of any animate or human forms, demonstrating that this region is selectively involved in the perception of faces.

A recent fMRI study on individuals with autism and Asperger syndrome showed a failure to activate the fusiform face area during face processing. Damage to fusiform gyrus and to amygdala results in impaired face recognition [24,25].

Parts of the inferior and medial temporal cortex may work together to process faces. For example, the anterior inferior temporal cortex and the superior temporal sulcus project to the lateral nucleus of the amygdala, with the amygdala responsible for assigning affective significance to faces, and thus affecting both attention and mnemonic aspects of face processing [26,27].

Behavioral studies suggest that the most salient parts for face recognition are, in order of importance, eyes, mouth, and nose [28].

Eye-scanning studies in humans and monkeys show that eyes and hair/forehead are scanned more frequently than the nose [29,30], while human infants focus on the eyes rather than the mouth [31]. Using eye-tracking technology to measure visual fixations, Klin [32] recently reported that adults with autism show abnormal patterns of attention when viewing naturalistic social scenes. These patterns include reduced attention to the eyes and increased attention to mouths, bodies, and objects.

3   Information Processing

The high specialization of specific brain areas for face analysis and recognition motivates the relevance of faces for social relations. On the other hand, this suggests that face understanding is not a low level process but involves higher level functional areas in the brain. These, in turn, must rely on a rich series of low level processes applied to enhance and extract face- specific features.

Among these processes it is possible to define:

- o **Face detection and tracking**. This process may involve the analysis of dynamic as well as geometric and photometric data on the retinal projection of the face.

- o **Facial features extraction**. Facial features are not simply distinctive points on the segmented face, but rather a collection of image features representing specific (and anatomically stable) areas of the face such as the eyes, eyebrows, ears, mouth, nostrils etc. Other, non-standard, subject-specific features are also included, such as the most famous Marilyn Monroe's naevus.

- o **Face image registration and warping**. Humans can easily recognize faces which are rotated and distorted up to a limited extent. The increase in time reported for recognition of rotated and distorted faces implies: the expectation on the geometric arrangement of facial features, and a specific process to organize the features (analogous to image registration and warping) before the actual recognition process can take place.

- o **Feature matching**. This process involves the comparison between the extracted set of facial features and the same set stored in the brain. The two process of feature extraction and matching (or memory recall) are not completely separated and sequential. From the eye scan paths recorded during face recognition experiments, it seems that, after moving the eyes over few general facial features, the gaze is directed toward subject-specific features, probably to enforce the expected identity.

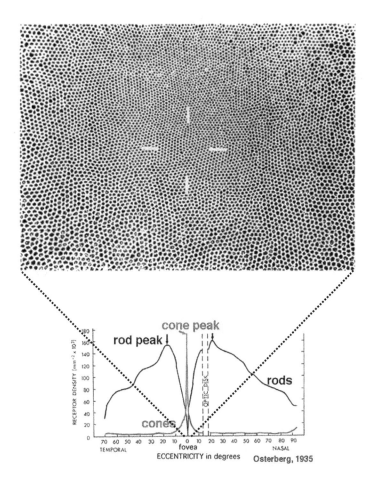

Fig. 2: Spatial organization of sensory elements in the human retina. (Top) Picture of the cones in the fovea centralis. (bottom) Diagram of the spatial distribution of the photoreceptors in the retina.

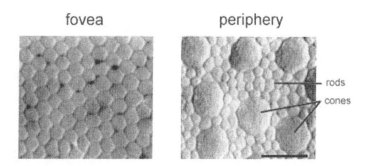

Fig. 3. Comparison of the spatial arrangement and size of the cones in the fovea and in the periphery.

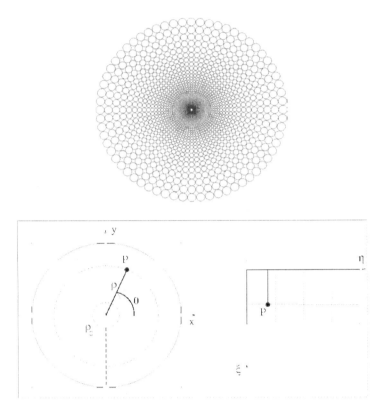

Fig. 4. Design of a space-variant imaging topology for image re-mapping. (Top) Actual layout of the log-polar sampling applied to images. (Bottom) Schematic representation of the log-polar transformation and the associated coordinate systems.

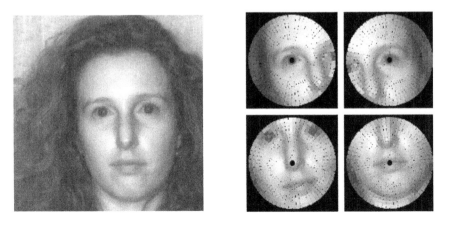

Fig. 5. Extraction of space-variant fixations. a) Original face image. b) Log-polar fixations extracted from (a).

From these processes higher level reasoning is possible, not only to determine the subject's identity, but also to understand more abstract elements (even uncorrelated to the subject's identity) which characterize the observed person (age, race, gender, emotion etc.).

Together with the defined general visual processes, the understanding of more abstract terms also requires the intervention of task-specific processes, such as motion analysis and facial features tracking for understanding emotion-specific patterns [4, 6, 7, 33-35].

As it is beyond the scope of this paper to trace all face-specific information processing, we will concentrate on face recognition and authentication, which not only are among the most studied aspects related to visual processing, but probably the most representative of the tasks involved in face image analysis.

4 Sensor Topologies and Spiral Grids

To achieve any visual task, including face recognition, humans are able to purposively control the flow of input data limiting the amount of information gathered from the sensory system [36-38]. This is needed to reduce the space and computation time required to process the incoming information.

It seems that every natural system is designed to minimize the amount of energy spent to achieve its goals. The minimal energy policy not only influences the processes and activities of living systems, more often related to survival, but also the mechanisms determining the geometrical structure of natural systems themselves. There are many examples in nature where the geometry of the system is specifically designed to limit the amount of space required to store/organize its elements. In many cases it seems that spiral topologies are the best suited geometric arrangements to allow an optimal (space saving) distribution of the elements in space. Some examples are depicted in figure 1.

The anatomy of the early stages of the human visual system is a clear example: despite the formidable acuity in the fovea centralis (1 minute of arc) and the wide field of view (about 140x200 degrees of solid angle), the optic nerve is composed of only 10^6 nerve fibres. The space-variant distribution of the ganglion cells in the retina allows a formidable data flow reduction. In fact, the same resolution would result in a space-invariant sensor of about $6x10^8$ pixels, thus resulting in a compression ratio of 1:600 [39].

The probability density of the spatial distribution of the ganglion cells, which convey the signal from the retinal layers to the optic nerve and is responsible for the data compression, follows a logarithmic-polar law. The number of cells decreases from the centre of the retina toward the periphery, with the maximal resolution in the fovea [40]. The same data compression can be obtained on electronic images, either by using a specially designed space-variant sensor [41], or re-sampling a standard image according to the log-polar transform [38,39].

The analytical formulation of the log-polar mapping describes the mapping that occurs between the retina (retinal plane (ρ, θ)) and the visual cortex (log-polar or cortical plane (ξ, η)). The derived logarithmic-polar law, taking into account the linear increment in size of the receptive fields, from the central region (fovea) towards the periphery, is given by:

$$\begin{cases} x = \rho \sin \theta \\ y = \rho \cos \theta \end{cases} \quad \begin{cases} \xi = \log_a (\rho/\rho_0) \\ \eta = q\theta \end{cases} \tag{1}$$

where a defines the amount of overlap among neighboring receptive fields, ρ_0 is the radius of the innermost circle, $1/q$ is the minimum angular resolution of the log-polar layout, and (ρ, θ) are the polar coordinates.

Other models for space-variant image geometries have been proposed, like the truncated pyramid [42], the reciprocal wedge transform (RWT) [43] and the complex logarithmic mapping (CLM) [44].

Several implementations of space-variant imaging have been developed: space-variant sensors [41], custom designed image re-sampling hardware [45], and special software routines [38,46]. Given the high processing power of current computing hardware, image re-mapping can be performed at frame rate without the need of special computing hardware, and also allows the use of conventional, low cost, cameras.

Space-variant image geometries have been applied to a variety of tasks, such as: visual tracking, form and object recognition, computation of stereo disparity and optical flow, depth perception and robot navigation [14].

More recently space-variant imaging has been applied to facilitate recognition with different biometric modalities [46,47]. A remarkable example is the Iris Scan iris recognition system patented by John Daugman [49]. The iris is firstly filtered by a bank of Gabor filters, then a set of features are extracted along a circular pattern following the rings of the iris. The extracted set of features are bitmapped to form a one-dimensional string of bits, the *IrisCode*, which is the template used to perform the matching. Bigun [50] proposed a space-variant sampling of face images to build a representation based on Gabor filtering for classification purposes. Log-polar fixations have been also used to perform face image matching [14]. More recently, Jain [51] applied a bank of Gabor filters, along a spiral grip, to capture both local and global details in a fingerprint as a compact fixed length FingerCode. The fingerprint matching is based on the Euclidean distance between the two corresponding *FingerCodes*.

5 Space-Variant Face Recognition

An important perceptual mechanism in humans is visual attention. Again, as not all visually available data is relevant for every given task, the human perceptual system is capable of making a selection of the input signal in various dimensions: "signal space" (low or high frequency data), depth (image areas corresponding to objects close or far from the observer), motion (static or moving objects) etc. The selection is

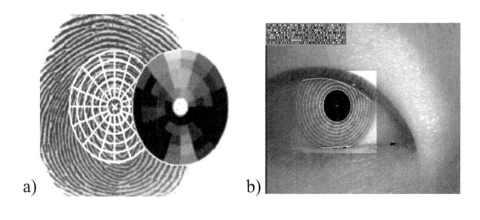

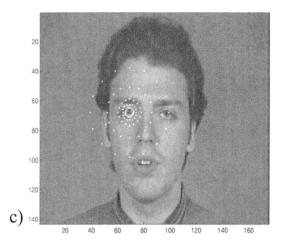

Fig. 6. Examples of spiral biometric representations. (a) Sample fingerprint and the extracted finger-code [51]. (b) Close up image of an eye and the circular pattern applied to extract the Iris-code [49]. (c) Log-polar pattern used to apply a Gabor decomposition of the facial features for face recognition [50].

controlled by a proper attention mechanism through ad-hoc band-limiting or focusing processes, which determine the areas of interest in the scene to which direct the gaze [48].

Given the abundance of data in a face image, both space-variant image re-sampling and the adoption of a selective attention mechanism can greatly improve the performance of recognition/authentication algorithms. The algorithms described for face authentication exploit these principles by extracting few pre-determined areas within the face and applying the matching to those image areas only. Processing face images these mechanisms must be tuned to the most salient features of the face itself.

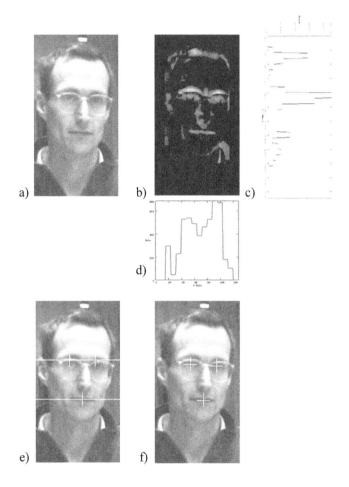

Fig. 7. Facial features detection. a) Original image. b) Valley image after morphological filtering. c) Cumulative values computed along the rows of (b). d) Cumulative values computed along the columns of the window identified by the maxima extracted from (c). e) First guess for the eyes and mouth position. f) Final position of the facial features computed by template matching around the estimation in (e).

5.1   Extraction of Facial Features

A technique applied to detect the facial features relies on the application of morphological operators to enhance structured iconic data such as contours, valleys and peaks in the gray levels. This information is gathered to make hypotheses for the presence of specific facial features. For example, the visible part of the sclera of the eye corresponds to a peak in the gray levels while the nostrils correspond to valleys. The position of the facial features is determined in two steps:

- by first computing the cumulative values of the filtered image along the rows. The eyes and mouth correspond to the areas with higher cumulative values; the mouth is assumed to lie in the area below the eyes;

- the same process is performed along the columns in the area corresponding to the eyes, determined at the previous step. The two maxima correspond to the horizontal position of the two eyes.

In order to avoid false matches a geometrical constraint is enforced to the position of the eyes and mouth, which is to lie at the vertexes of a triangle. The values assumed by the angles of the triangle are bounded by values determined experimentally ($44° < \alpha_i < 84°$).

The exact position of the features is determined by computing the cross-correlation between the image and a feature template, within a 10x10 pixels window centered on the previously determined position. The template is obtained by cutting the eyes and mouth out of a sample image of the same subject. From an extensive test this choice demonstrated to give more accurate results than computing an average template. This is due to the fact that the averaging process deforms considerably the feature's shape degrading the matching results.

The three correlation values stemming from the eyes and mouth are averaged to obtain a score between −1 and 1. If the geometric constraint is satisfied and the matching score is higher than a given threshold the fixations are considered as valid ones. In order to determine the discriminant value for the correlation score, a validation test has been performed on a set of 2019 images completely uncorrelated from the recognition database. These images have been divided into two classes: all images (1609) where the facial features are partially occluded or not visible, plus all the images where the mean difference between the estimated and the manually determined feature positions is greater than a given threshold[1]; all remaining images in the set (410).

The FAR and FRR test values were computed from the feature correlation scores of the two image sets. These statistical measures represent the capability of separating the two classes, valid and wrong features. The score value corresponding to equal FAR and FRR determines the reliability of the estimated features.

5.2 Analysis of Matching Techniques

Two matching techniques are presented. In the former, the subject is represented by a collection of fixations from the face image. The matching is performed by computing the correlation between the representation of the reference subject and the acquired face image. The algorithm is based on the following steps:

1. Given the position of selected facial features (the eyes and the mouth), three log-polar fixations are extracted from the acquired image of the subject (see figure 5).
2. The log-polar images are warped to simulate views as close as possible to the pose and orientation of the reference subject's face (almost parallel to the image plane).

---

[1] This threshold is determined statistically by computing the probability of locating the facial features correctly in more than 50% in a given image ensemble.

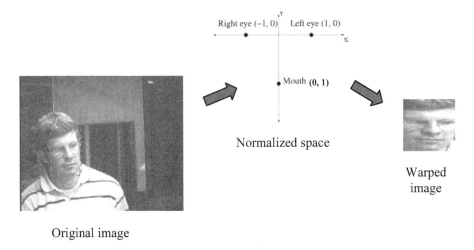

Fig. 8. Extraction of the face window and warping.

3. Corresponding fixations are compared by computing the sum of the absolute values of gray level differences[2] and the normalized correlation. Two matching scores are obtained from each fixation independently.
4. The scores obtained by the log-polar fixations are combined to form a 6 components vector representing the similarity between the subject and the model.

The log-polar transformation is computed at frame rate by using special re-mapping software routines. The feature extraction and matching processes may be iterated over other subject-independent (like the eyebrows) or subject-dependent features, thus increasing the reliability of the recognition process.

The latter technique performs the matching over a single window containing the whole face [52]. As a major problem with template matching is the registration of the two images, the window is warped according to a feature space determined by the position of the facial features (see figure 3). A simpler technique performs the matching on just a single window containing the whole face in Cartesian coordinates. As a major problem with template matching is the registration of the two images, the window is warped according to a feature space determined by the position of the facial features. Therefore, in this case, the facial features are not used to extract sub-windows out of the subject's face but rather to align and scale the face with the model image [52].

---

[2] To compute the difference, the gray levels of each log-polar fixation are first normalized to the range of intensity values of the corresponding facial feature of the reference subject.

Fig. 9. Sample images recorded from the industrial database.

Fig. 10. Sample images from the database acquired in our laboratory.

6 Evaluation of Matching Techniques

Every face matching scheme is devised to deliver a similarity score from each compared image-template pair. From the computed scores a statistical classifier can be used to determine the similarity between a given model and the subject.

The described algorithms were tested on a subset (with, at least, two images for each subject) of the FERET database [6] yielding 2.5 EER for both methods [14]. The same tests were also performed on the Olivetti Resarch Lab database [55], using the five even images, out of the set of ten per subject, to simulate training, and the other five for testing. The matching result for each trial has been obtained using a max rule to combine the similarity scores, yielding 8.5% EER (performing full face matching).

In order to test the systems within a real scenario, two ad-hoc databases were collected. The former ("academic" database) is quite similar, in principle, to the FERET database [6]. The database contains 124 gray level images (8 bits) from 45 subjects, the image size is 512x512 pixels with approximately the same number of males and females.

To test the algorithms in the worst conditions, a more challenging database ("industrial" database) has been acquired, composed of 488 gray level images (8 bits per pixel) from 75 subjects. The image size is 384x288 pixels and the head size is always smaller than 80x120 pixels. This database as been acquired from a camera placed at the entrance of an industry working area. The subjects were completely unaware of the camera and, as a consequence, the faces within the pictures are quite different in size, facial expression, orientation and pose. Most of the pictures from the same subject were acquired at least days or even weeks apart. The resulting face database has so many unpredictable changes to make it a real challenge for any face matching technique.

The similarity measurements for the subjects in the databases are obtained from a complete matching over all the images in the data set (all subjects versus all images). Given M images for each of N subjects, the results obtained can be divided into two classes[3] (assuming, as a general rule, that more than a single score is available for each image comparison):

- matching scores obtained comparing all different images of the same subject, equal to $N \times M \times (M - 1)$ comparisons (*client tests*);

- matching scores obtained comparing all different images of different subjects, equal to $N \times M^2 - N \times (N + M - 1)$ comparisons (*impostor tests*);

A covariance matrix is defined describing each of the two classes:

$$\Sigma_i = \frac{1}{N_i} \sum_{j=1}^{N_i} \left(x_j^i - m_i \right)\left(x_j^i - m_i \right)^t \tag{2}$$

---

[3] As a consequence of the experimental procedure the training set and the test set are disjoint, except for the case where the image used to build the representation of one subject is also used for an impostor test.

where N_i represents the number of elements of class "i" and m_i is the mean value of the same class. Given the entire ensemble of matching scores for the two classes (each score can be regarded as a vector within the class), the discrimination power can be defined through five statistical indexes [52-54]:

- The intraset (R_1 and R_2) and interset(H) distances (class separability indexes).

- The Bayesian error probability.

- The false acceptance, false rejection and the equal error rate (FAR, FRR, EER).

The first two indexes define the distances among the elements of the same class and between the two classes. By comparing the two it is possible to define the separability between the two classes, e.g. to discriminate the set of clients from all the impostors.

Given the intraset distances R_1 and R_2, computed as the mean distances between all matching vector pairs[4] in the two classes, and the interset distance H, computed as the mean distance among all vectors in the two classes, for a good separation between the two classes the intraset distances are expected to be much smaller than the interset distance:

$$Q = \frac{R_1 + R_2}{H} \tag{3}$$

a low value of Q means the two classes are well separated.

Another separability measure is given by the Bhattacharrya distance [11]:

$$\beta = \int \sqrt{p\left(x/\omega_1\right) p\left(x/\omega_2\right)} \, dx \tag{4}$$

where x is the measurement vector, ω_1 and ω_2 represent the two classes. The resulting distance β is bounded between 0 and 1. If either of the two conditional probabilities $p(x/y)$ is equally zero, the two classes are very well separated, while if β is equal to zero the two classes are superimposed. Consequently, the smaller the value of β the higher the separability between the two classes.

Assuming the probability density of the measurements vectors to be Gaussian, it is possible to compute:

$$B = -\ln \beta = \frac{1}{8}(m_1 - m_2)^t \left(\frac{\Sigma_1 + \Sigma_2}{2}\right)^{-1}(m_1 - m_2) + \frac{1}{2}\ln\left(\frac{\left|\frac{1}{2}(\Sigma_1 + \Sigma_2)\right|}{\sqrt{(|\Sigma_1||\Sigma_2|)}}\right) \tag{5}$$

---

[4] A matching vector is defined as the set of matching scores obtained from the matching engine of the system. The vector can be composed of a single element, if the matching involves a single facial feature, or many elements

where m_1 and m_2 are the mean measurement vectors of the two classes (clients and impostors), Σ_1 and Σ_2 are the covariance matrices of the measurements of the two classes. The Bayesian error probability can be estimated from the Bhattacharrya distance as:

$$P_e \le \frac{1}{2}\beta \tag{6}$$

Most of the techniques applied to evaluate the similarity between the representation of two subjects rely on single distance measurements. In the presented method multiple fixations are used to represent the subject, yielding multiple distance measurements for each subject. In order to analyze the distribution of the client and impostor tests it is necessary to represent the probability densities as one-dimensional functions. The Fisher transform (a method for multivariate system analysis is) allows to project a vector function on a one-dimensional space. Through this technique it is possible to analyze the distributions of the measurement vectors of the two classes as two one-dimensional functions. The matching scores are used to compute the Fisher vector:

$$w = S_w^{-1}(m_1 - m_2)$$

$$S_w = S_1 + S_2 \ ; \ S_i = \sum_{j=1}^{N}(x_j^i - m_i)(x_j^i - m_i)^t \tag{7}$$

where N_1 and N_2 represent again the number of elements in each class and the other terms are defined as in the previous equations. The measurement vectors are projected on the Fisher's vector and the distribution of the two classes are computed. The resulting curves represent the probability densities of the missed clients and the allowed impostors, as a function of the matching score. The integrals of the two curves represent the FAR and FRR. From the resulting representation two results are inferred:

- The equal error rate of the system, which is the probability of equally accepting an impostor or rejecting a client. This measure is computed as the probability corresponding to the coordinate, on the horizontal axis, where the two probability density functions have the same area.

- The best discriminant threshold, which is the threshold to be applied to the computed matching scores to assure the best separation between the two classes. This is determined by the horizontal coordinate corresponding to the intersection point between the two curves.

Both these parameters define the goodness of the identity verification system, but the second one can also be applied as a threshold to perform recognition.

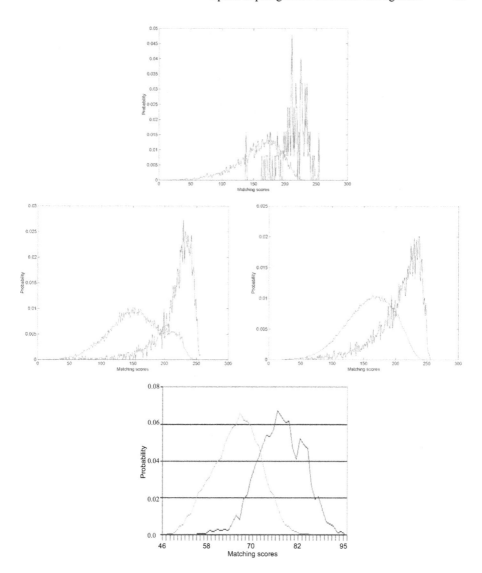

Fig. 11. Fisher distributions computed from the matching scores obtained from the two databases used in the experiments. (Top) distribution obtained computing the matching scores over space-variant fixations on the academic database. (Middle) Distributions obtained computing the matching on a single window centred on the industrial database. The distributions on the left is obtained from a subset of the database, the one on the right is related to the full database. (Bottom) Fisher distribution computed from a commercial system tested on the industrial database.

Among the many variables in the matching process we concentrated on the influence of the feature localization error. From the reported experiments it turns out that the system's performances are greatly influenced by the accuracy in the estimation of the position of facial features. In fact, two different methods were tested for feature detection: the former based on matching a generic template of the facial features, the latter applying a specific template extracted from the image of the model face, which correspond to the actual facial features of the subject to be recognized. The second approach effectively maximizes the probability of correct feature localization for the subject to be recognized.

From the obtained matching scores a simple recognition experiment has been attempted. Given a model image for each subject (or client), all other images matched with the five highest correlation scores (the same model image has not been matched with itself) were ranked. By applying a simple voting procedure, where the subject corresponding to the highest number of instances within the selected five is chosen, a remarkable 98% recognition rate was obtained. The remaining 2% was composed of subjects were all five selected images were from different individuals but still included at least one image of the client.

This last result confirms the need for a two-step matching strategy where an iconic matcher is firstly used to perform a rough separation between the two classes (clients and impostors) and selecting a set of possible candidates. The following stage can be an independent measurement, like a higher resolution and more localized matching, but performed only on the image set already selected.

Table 1. Performances of the face matching system described in section 4.2 The two columns in the middle report the computed error probability and the false acceptance/rejection with two different methods for the extraction of the facial features. As a reference, the last column reports the performances of a highly reputed commercial system.

	Subject-based template	Generic template	Commercial system based on LFA
Pe	30.5%	36.5%	31.5%
FAR	15%	25%	19.68%
FRR	17%	21.3%	20.34%

7 Conclusion

The analysis of faces is one of the most important visual processes in humans. From neurophysiology and psychofisics experiments it turns out that high level processes are devoted to the interpretation of face images. Several areas in the brain effectively cooperate to the selection and extraction of face-related features for recognition. In particular, parts of the inferior and medial temporal cortex may work together to process faces. Based on these findings it is possible to postulate that distinctive features, both subject-dependent and subject-independent, are used to perform recognition. On the other hand this is not a serial process, as implicit in many computer-based recognition systems, but rather a parallel process where recognition is performed while the features are extracted. As more features are detected and extracted, the confidence in recognition is improved. The model of face analysis, as learned from neurophisiology, can be applied as the basic scheme for an information system to process face images.

Given this basic computational scheme, the concept of fixation is fundamental for recognition. As in many natural systems the spatial distribution of image elements is crucial because it determines the image resolution and the amount of information conveyed by each single fixation. Resolution and the amount of information are not always linearly dependent: the same amount of information can be represented with a small resolution given a proper spatial organization of the picture elements. For this reason many natural systems adopt a spiral, space-variant distribution of their elements to maximize the amount of information with a "minimal energy" representation. To incorporate this concept within a biometric system is straightforward. Several examples exist in the literature where space-variant representations have been used even for non-facial biometrics. Two remarkable examples are the iris-code designed for iris recognition and the finger-code applied to fingerprint recognition.

An iconic matching algorithm, based on the analysis of fixations, has been considered and stressed to the worst possible working conditions by using an ad-hoc database. The aim was to understand the actual limits and failing modes not only of the specific method applied, but also of any general iconic-based matching technique.

From the error indices reported in this, as well as previous papers [40,41], it is possible to make the following considerations:

- The face registration and/or warping step is critical for the entire recognition process. Space-variant representations implicitly enforce a high spatial localization of features. In fact, small displacement induce big differences on the image.

- The performances of an identity verification system cannot be assessed with a trial on a data set only, but multiple and different data sets are necessary to understand the real failing modes. For this reason the proposed system has been tested on several databases.

- There is an intrinsic limit, also statistically demonstrated, in using a matching technique alone to discriminate a set of given clients from the class of all possible impostors.

The clear limitations of a single matching engine in making a discrimination among thousands of images, enforces the need for either a multi-level or a multi-algorithmic process, where several (at least two) cooperating "experts" are applied to the same authentication process.

Several aspects have been addressed explicitly but many are still under investigation. In this paper the analysis has been restricted to a simple image representation, but further work can be done by matching multiple features either at the first level or at the second processing level.

References

[1] R. Chellappa, C.L. Wilson, and S. Sirohey. "Human and machine recognition of faces: A survey". *Proceedings of the IEEE*, Vol. 83, pp 705-740, 1995.

[2] T. Kanade. *Computer recognition of human faces*. Birkhauser, Basel and Stuttgart, 1977.

[3] P. Sinha and T. Poggio. "I think I know that face...". *Nature*, Vol. 384, pp. 404, 1996.

[4] L. Wiskott, J.M. Fellous, N. Kruger and C. von der Malsburg. "Face recognition and gender determination". In *Proceedings Int.l Workshop on Automatic Face and Gesture Recognition*, pp. 92-97, Zurich, Switzerland, 1995.

[5] Anil K. Jain, Ruud Bolle, Sharath Pankanti. *Biometrics, Personal Identification in Networked Society*, Kluwer Academic Publishers, 1999

[6] H. Wechsler, P. Phillips,V. Bruce, F. Soulie, and T. Huang (Eds.), *Face Recognition. From Theory to Applications*, NATO ASI Series F, Vol. 163, Springer-Verlag, Berlin Heidelberg.

[7] G. Cottrell and J. Metcalfe. "Face, gender and emotion recognition using holons". In D. Touretzky, editor, *Advances in Neural Information Processing Systems*, Vol. 3, pages 564-571, San Mateo, CA, 1991. Morgan Kaufmann.

[8] P.N. Belhumeur, J.P. Hespanha, and D.J. Kriegman. "Eigenfaces vs. fisherfaces: Recognition using class specific linear projection". *IEEE Trans. on PAMI*, PAMI-19(7):711-20, 1997.

[9] G.J. Edwards, T.F. Cootes and C.J. Taylor. "Face Recognition Using Active Appearance Models". In *Proc. of 5th European Conference on Computer Vision*, pp 581-95, Springer Verlag, 1998.

[10] R. Brunelli and T. Poggio. "Face recognition through geometrical features". In *Proc. of 2nd European Conference on Computer Vision*, pp 792-800, S. Margherita Ligure (Italy), 1992. Springer Verlag.

[11] B. Mogbaddam, T. Jebara and A. Pentland. "Bayesian face recognition". *Pattern Recognition*, 33(11):1771-82, Nov. 2000.

[12] G.C. Feng, P.C. Yuen, and D.Q. Dai. "Human face recognition using pca on wavelet subband". *Journal of Electronic Imaging*, 9(2):226--33, 2000.

[13] C. Liu and H. Wechsler. "Evolutionary pursuit and its application to face recognition". *IEEE Transaction on PAMI*, 22(6):570-582, 2000.

[14] M. Tistarelli and E. Grosso. "Active vision-based face authentication". *Image and Vision Computing: Special issue on Facial Image Analysis*, M. Tistarelli ed., Vol. 18, no. 4, pp 299-314, 2000.

[15] C. Darwin. *The expression of the emotions in man and animals*. London, U.K.: John Murray, 1965. (Original work published 1872)

[16] C. Goren, M. Sarty and P. Wu. "Visual following and pattern discrimination of face-like stimuli by newborn infants". *Pediatrics, 56*, 544–549, 1975.

[17] G. E. Walton and T. G. R. Bower. "Newborns form "prototypes" in less than 1 minute". *Psychological Science, 4*, 203–205, 1993.

[18] J. Fagan. "Infants' recognition memory for face". *Journal of Experimental Child Psychology, 14*, 453–476, 1972.

[19] M. de Haan and C. A. Nelson. "Recognition of the mother's face by 6-month-old infants: A neurobehavioral study". *Child Development, 68*, 187–210, 1997.

[20] C. M. Leonard, E. T. Rolls, F. A. W. Wilson and G. C. Baylis. "Neurons in the amygdala of the monkey with responses selective for faces". *Behavioral Brain Research, 15*, 159–176, 1985.

[21] I. Gauthier, M. J. Tarr, A. W. Anderson, P. Skudlarski and J. C. Gore. "Activation of the middle fusiform "face area" increases with expertise in recognizing novel objects". *Nature Neuroscience, 2*, 568–573, 1999.

[22] N. Kanwisher, J. McDermott and M. M. Chun. "The fusiform face area: A module in human extrastriate cortex specialized for face perception". *Journal of Neuroscience, 17*, 4302–4311, 1997.

[23] G. McCarthy, A. Puce, J. C. Gore and T. Allison. "Facespecific processing in the human fusiform gyrus". *Journal of Cognitive Neuroscience, 8*, 605–610, 1997.

[24] R. T. Schultz, I. Gauthier, A. Klin, R. K. Fulbright, A. W. Anderson, F. R. Volkmar, P. Skudlarski, C. Lacadie, D. J. Cohen and J. C. Gore. "Abnormal ventral temporal cortical activity during face discrimination among individuals with autism and Asperger syndrome". *Archives of General Psychiatry, 57*, 331–340, 2000.

[25] A. R. Damasio, J. Damasio and G. W. Van Hoesen. "Prosopagnosia: Anatomic basis and behavioral mechanisms". *Neurology, 32*, 331–341, 1982.

[26] C. A. Nelson. "The development and neural bases of face recognition". *Infant and Child Development, 10*, 3-18, 2001.

[27] J. P. Aggleton, M. J. Burton and R. E. Passingham. "Cortical and subcortical afferents to the amygdala of the rhesus monkey (*Macaca mulatta*)". *Brain Research, 190*, 347–368, 1980.

[28] J. Shepherd. "Social factors in face recognition". In G. Davies, H. Ellis & J. Shepherd (Eds.), *Perceiving and remembering faces* (pp. 55–79). London: Academic Press, 1981.

[29] A. L. Yarbus. *Eye movements and vision*. New York: Plenum Press, 1967.

[30] F. K. D. Nahm, , A. Perret, D. Amaral, and T. D. Albright. "How do monkeys look at faces?" *Journal of Cognitive Neuroscience, 9*, 611–623, 1997.

[31] M. M. Haith,., T. Bergman, and M. J. Moore. "Eye contact and face scanning in early infancy". *Science, 198*, 853–854, 1979.

[32] A. Klin. "Eye-tracking of social stimuli in adults with autism*"*. NICHD Collaborative Program of Excellence in Autism. Yale University, New Haven, CT, May 2001.

[33] B. Braathen and M. S. Bartlett and G. Littlewort and J. R. Movellan. "First Steps Towards Automatic Recognition of Spontaneous Facial Action Units" *ACM Workshop on Perceptive User Interfaces,* Orlando (FL), Nov. 15-16 2001.

[34] Picard, R.W.. "Toward computers that recognize and respond to user emotion". IBM System,(39), 3/4, 2000.

[35] Picard, R.W. "Building HAL: Computers that sense, recognize, and respond to human emotion". MIT Media-Lab TR-532. *Also in* Society of Photo-Optical Instrumentation Engineers. Human Vision and Electronic Imaging VI, part of IS&T/SPIE9s Photonics West, 2001.

[36] D.H. Ballard. "Animate vision". *Artificial Intelligence*, Vol. 48, pp. 57-86, 1991.

[37] Y. Aloimonos (Ed.). "Purposive, qualitative, active vision". *CVGIP: Image Understanding*, 56(special issue on qualitative, active vision), Vol. 56, July 1992.

[38] M. Tistarelli. "Active/space-variant object recognition". Image and Vision Computing, 13(3):215-226, 1995.

[39] E. L. Schwartz, D. N. Greve, and G. Bonmassar. "Space-variant active vision: definition, overview and examples". Neural Networks, Vol. 8, No. 7/8, pp. 1297-1308, 1995.

[40] C. A. Curcio, K. R. Sloan, R. E. Kalina, A. E. Hendrickson. "Human photoreceptor topography". J Comp Neurol., vol. 292, no. 4, 497-523, 1990.

[41] G. Sandini, G. Metta. "Retina- like sensors: motivations, technology and applications". In Sensors and Sensing in Biology and Engineering. T.W. Secomb, F. Barth, and P. Humphrey (Eds). Springer-Verlag. 2002

[42] P. J. Burt, Smart sensing in machine vision". In Machine Vision: Algorithms, Architectures, and Systems, Academic Press, 1988.

[43] F. Tong, Ze-Nian Li. "Reciprocal-wedge transform for space-variant sensing". IEEE Transactions on PAMI, Vol. 17, 500-511, 1995

[44] E. L. Schwartz. "Spatial mapping in the primate sensory projection: Analytic structure and relevance to perception", Biological Cybernetics, vol. 25, 181-194, 1977.

[45] T.E. Fisher and R.D. Juday. "A programmable video image remapper", In Proc. of SPIE, vol. 938, 122-128, 1988

[46] E. Grosso, M. Tistarelli. "Log-polar Stereo for Anthropomorphic Robots". In Proc. of 6th European Conference on Computer Vision, LNCS 1842, Springer Verlag, 299-313, 2000

[47] G. Sandini and M. Tistarelli. "Vision and space-variant sensing". In H. Wechsler (Ed), Neural Networks for Perception: Human and Machine Perception, Academic Press, 1991

[48] Y. Yeshurun and E.L. Schwartz. Shape description with a space-variant sensor: Algorithms for scan-path, fusion and convergence over multiple scans". IEEE Transactions on PAMI, vol. 11, 1217-1222, Nov. 1989

[49] J. Daugman. "High confidence visual recognition of persons by a test of statistical independence". IEEE Transactions on PAMI, vol. 15, no. 11, 1148-1161, 1993

[50] J. Bigun. "Retinal vision applied to facial features detection and face authentication". Pattern Recognition Letters, vol. 23, no. 4, 463-475, 1997

[51] K. Jain, S. Prabhakar, L. Hong, S. Pankanti. "Filterbank-based fingerprint matching". IEEE Transactions on IP, vol. 9, no. 5, 846-859, 2000

[52] M. Tistarelli, A. Lagorio, and E. Grosso. "Understanding Iconic Image-Based Face Biometrics". Proc. of Int.l Workshop on Biometric Authentication, Copenaghen, Denmark, Springer Verlag, LNCS 2359, 19-29, 202

[53] M. Tistarelli, A. Lagorio, and E. Grosso. "Image-Based techniques for biometric authentication". Proc. of Int.l Conference on Multimedia and Expo, special session on Biometrics: New Challenges for User Authentification, Lausanne, Switzerland, August 22-26, 2002

[54] Grother P.J. "Cross validation comparison of NIST ocr databases". In Proceedings of the SPIE, volume 1906, 296-307, 1993

[55] Samaria, F., Harter, A.: Parameterisation of a Stochastic Model for Human Face Identification. In Proceedings of 2nd IEEE Workshop on Applications of Computer Vision, Sarasota, FL. IEEE Computer Society Press, 1994

Statistical Learning Approaches with Application to Face Detection

Emanuele Franceschi, Francesca Odone, and Alessandro Verri

INFM - DISI, Università di Genova, Genova (I)

Abstract. We present a concise tutorial on statistical learning, the theoretical ground on which the learning from examples paradigm is based. We also discuss the problem of face detection as a case study illustrating the solutions proposed in this framework. Finally, we describe some new results we obtained by means of an object detection method based on statistical hypothesis tests which makes use of positive examples only.

1 Introduction

Over the years long standing recognition problems of computer vision research have been approached with a broad spectrum of techniques. On one end of the spectrum one finds geometric methods in which recognition takes place if the obtained description matches the geometric model. On the other end trainable methods build a solution from a given set of examples. Not surprisingly, practical solutions fall in the middle attempting to combine the strengths of these two rather extreme views. Face detection is a prototypical example since in the literature one finds many different approaches to the problem effectively exploring the entire spectrum — see for example [3, 13, 36].

Here, starting from a description of recent advances in the learning from examples approach we summarize some of the most up-to-date techniques for face detection and present some new results obtained in the particular case in which only positive examples are used.

2 A Brief Tutorial on Statistical Learning

In this short introduction to statistical learning theory we follow the seminal works in [30, 31, 8, 6]. Additional material on Support Vector Machines can be found in [5], while for a broader introduction we refer to [10].

2.1 Setting the Notation and the Problem

Statistical learning is emerging as a key methodology for dealing with a vast class of problems aiming at finding a relation between inputs and outputs. The application domains include computer vision and speech understanding, computer graphics, text and document classification, bioinformatics, and time series prediction.

M. Tistarelli, J. Bigun, and E. Grosso (Eds.): Biometrics School 2003, LNCS 3161, pp. 91–104, 2005.

In the typical setting one considers two random variables $\mathbf{x} \in X \subset \mathbb{R}^d$, the input, and $y \in Y \subset \mathbb{R}$, the output, related by a probabilistic relationship. Given a data set $D_\ell \equiv \{(\mathbf{x}_i, y_i) \in X \times Y\}_{i=1}^{\ell}$ *training set*, obtained by sampling ℓ times the set $X \times Y$ according to a certain probability distribution $p(\mathbf{x}, y)$, the key problem of statistical learning consists in finding a function $f : X \to Y$ that can be used to predict a value y for each $\mathbf{x} \in X$, given D_ℓ. The ideal solution is defined as the minimizer of a measure of the expected error, the so called *expected risk*, defined as

$$I[f] \equiv \int_{X,Y} V(y, f(\mathbf{x}))p(\mathbf{x}, y) \; d\mathbf{x}dy,$$

where V is some *loss function* measuring the price to pay predicting $f(\mathbf{x})$ in place of y.

The minimizer of $I[f]$, f_0, often called *target function*, belongs to some space $\mathcal{F}$ and cannot be found in practice, because the probability distribution $p(\mathbf{x}, y)$ is unknown. In practice, using the data set D_ℓ one can build an approximation of the expected risk, called *empirical risk* [31], defined as

$$I_{\text{emp}}[f; \ell] = \frac{1}{\ell} \sum_{i=1}^{\ell} V(y_i, f(\mathbf{x}_i)).$$

The minimizer of the empirical risk can be thought of as an approximation to the ideal estimator. However, the minimization of the empirical risk in $\mathcal{F}$ is not unique (a typical example of ill-posed problem) and, if the solution space is too large, might lead to overfitting.

In order to avoid overfitting, statistical learning studies solutions for which the distance between the empirical and expected risk is bounded through inequalities of the type

$$I[f] < I_{}[f] + \varphi\left(\sqrt{\frac{h}{\ell}}, \eta\right), \tag{1}$$

where φ is an increasing function of h/ℓ and η and the bound holds true with probability at least η for all functions in a certain space, called *hypothesis space*, in which the empirical risk can be minimized uniquely. The quantity h measures the capacity of the hypothesis space and is the key to control overfit. For more details and examples of capacity measures and exact forms of φ we refer the reader to [32, 14, 31, 1].

2.2 Regularization Networks

As proposed in [7, 31], instead of minimizing the empirical risk, one looks for the optimal trade off between the empirical risk and the capacity of the hypothesis space as suggested by inequality (1). This observation leads to the principle of *Structural Risk Minimization*.

Alternatively, [34] considers hypothesis spaces which are Reproducing Kernel Hilbert Spaces (RKHS). An RKHS is a Hilbert space of functions f of the form $f(\mathbf{x}) = \sum_{n=1}^{N} a_n \phi_n(\mathbf{x})$, where $\{\phi_n(\mathbf{x})\}_{n=1}^{N}$ is a set of linearly independent basis functions and N is not necessarily finite. The norm of a function f in an RKHS is defined as:

$$\|f\|_K^2 = \sum_{n=1}^{N} \frac{a_n^2}{\lambda_n},$$

where $\{\lambda_n\}_{n=1}^{N}$ is a decreasing sequence of strictly positive real numbers such that

$$\sum_{n=1}^{N} \lambda_n < +\infty.$$

It is then easy to show that the λ_n and the basis functions $\{\phi_n\}_{n=1}^{N}$ define the symmetric positive definite kernel function:

$$K(\mathbf{x}, \mathbf{y}) = \sum_{n=1}^{N} \lambda_n \phi_n(\mathbf{x}) \phi_n(\mathbf{y}).$$

If we define an hypothesis space H as

$$H = \{f \in \text{RKHS} : \|f\|_K \leq A\},$$

it can be shown that the capacity of H is an increasing function of A (see for example [8]). The solution of the learning problem is found by searching for the minimum of functionals like

$$\Phi[f] = \frac{1}{\ell} \sum_{i=1}^{\ell} V(y_i, f(\mathbf{x}_i)) + \lambda \|f\|_K^2. \tag{2}$$

This can be viewed as an example of regularization of an ill posed problem where uniqueness is achieved by finding the optimal trade off between the data term, the empirical risk, and the *smoothness* term, $\|f\|_K^2$ re λ is a positive parameter controlling the relative weight. For a fixed λ, the regularized solution can be thought of as the function of minimum RKHS norm approximating the data within some degree of accuracy. A discussion linking structural risk minimization to regularization networks can be found in [8].

An important feature of the minimizer of $\Phi[f]$ is that for a broad range of loss functions the minimizer has the same general form [34]

$$f(\mathbf{x}) = \sum_{i=1}^{\ell} \alpha_i K(\mathbf{x}, \mathbf{x}_i). \tag{3}$$

Spline approximation and Radial Basis Functions are examples of this scheme [9, 31].

2.3   Support Vector Machines and Related Schemes

In this section we discuss a few learning techniques based on the minimization of functionals of the form (2) and on the choice of different loss functions. Different V lead to different learning techniques, and thus to different learning algorithms for computing the coefficients α_i in (3).

Linear approximation schemes arise from the minimization of the functional in (2) with the quadratic loss function V defined as

$$V(y, f(\mathbf{x})) = (y - f(\mathbf{x}))^2.$$

In these cases the coefficients α_i in (3) satisfy the following linear system of equations [9])

$$(K + \lambda I)\boldsymbol{\alpha} = \mathbf{y},$$

where I is the identity matrix, $\mathbf{y} = (y_1, ..., y_\ell)$, $\boldsymbol{\alpha} = (\alpha_1, ..., \alpha_\ell)$, and $K_{ij} = K(\mathbf{x}_i, \mathbf{x}_j)$.

In the case of Support Vector Machines (SVM) [4, 31] we distinguish between real output (regression) and binary output (classification) problems. The scheme of SVM for classification is obtained through the loss function V

$$V(y, f(\mathbf{x})) = (1 - yf(\mathbf{x}))_+, \tag{4}$$

where $(t)_+ = \max\{0, t\}$. In the case of classification the solution is given by the sign of Eq. (3). SVMs for regression are based, instead, on the loss function V, called ϵ-insensitive loss

$$V(y, f(\mathbf{x})) = |y - f(\mathbf{x})|_\epsilon, \tag{5}$$

where $|t|_\epsilon \equiv \max\{0, |t| - \epsilon\}$.

In both cases, the coefficients α_i can be found by solving a Quadratic Programming (QP) problem with linear constraints. The regularization parameter λ appears only in the linear constraints: for each coefficient α_i $0 \leq \alpha_i \leq 1/(2\lambda\ell)$. A number of algorithms for training SVM have been proposed: some are based on a decomposition approach where the QP problem is attacked by solving a sequence of smaller QP problems [19], others on sequential updates of the solution [22].

We conclude this section with two important comments. First, we notice that a remarkable property of SVMs is that both loss functions lead to *sparse* solutions, i.e., unlike in the case of linear approximation methods, typically only a small fraction of the coefficients α_i in the expansion (3) are nonzero (the data points $\mathbf{x}_i$ associated with the nonzero α_i are called *support vectors*). The sparsity of the solution means that if one discards all the data points that are not support vectors, the same solution is found. One can immediately see that SVMs have interesting data compression properties: the support vectors represent the most informative data points and carry all the information contained in the training set, thus all the other training examples could be discarded.

Second, it can be shown that, in classification, the inverse of the RKHS norm equals the *margin* [31], a quantity measuring the distance of the closest point in the training set from the separating surface. Therefore, an SVM looks for a separating surface which leaves the closest point as far as possible by controlling the norm (i.e., the smoothness) of the solution.

3   Face Detection

Face detection is an active area of research (see, for instance, [16, 35, 24, 23, 26, 33] or the surveys [3, 13, 36]). In this brief description on the state-of-the-art we consider face detection methods for single image, and focus on example-based face detection. In this field many approaches have been proposed, ranging from eigenfaces [29], Neural Networks [24, 25], SVM classifiers trained on whole faces [20, 21] and on face components [11, 18], systems based on Adaboost [33, 17], Naive Bayes Classifiers [26]. Here we describe some of the most interesting achievements presented in recent years.

In [21] is presented an example-based learning system for object detection in the context of face, people, and car detection. The system uses Haar wavelet features as inputs to a SVM classifier. In the training step, the system takes a set of aligned and normalized images of the object class (positive examples) and a set of patterns that do not belong to the object class (negative examples). Haar wavelet features are computed for each pattern and then an SVM is trained to distinguish between positive and negative examples. In the testing phase, the system slides a fixed size window over a test image and uses the trained classifier to decide whether a window show the objects of interest. In the described system the whole object was represented by one feature vector which is fed into a single classifier.

More recently, in [12], a component-based approach is proposed. The object to detect is decomposed into a set of components that are interconnected by a flexible geometrical model. The results show that this system performs better for detecting objects when varying the viewing conditions, since each component varies less under pose changes than the pattern belonging to the whole object. The authors developed a two-level classification system that implies geometrical relations between components. On the first level, component linear SVM classifiers independently detect components of the face. On the second level, the classifier checks if the geometrical configuration of the detected components corresponds with the learned geometrical model of a face. For what concerns the choice of the components, instead of selecting eyes, mouth, and nose that are specialized for the face detection application, they designed a more general method that automatically determines selective rectangular components from a set of synthetic face images.

Viola and Jones [33] propose a face detection system based on AdaBoost. They represent image windows as a collection of features called *rectangle features* (inspired by Haar Wavelets) and train a weak classifier for each feature. Since each weak classifier is based on a single rectangle feature, the AdaBoost procedure works in this case as a feature selector. At each iteration only the feature performing best — i.e., producing smaller number of errors on the training set compared to the others — is added to the final strong classifier. The authors achieve state-of-the-art results with this method, and also present a way of combining the classifiers that they call "cascade" that allows fast elimination of background regions and therefore fast detection.

4   A Method Based on Hypothesis Testing

In this section we describe a novel methodology for detecting faces in images which is heavily based on hypothesis testing mechanisms.

Classical nonparametric statistical approaches (see [15] for a quite complete overview of this subject) are perhaps less popular within the computer vision community than Bayesian and/or statistical learning techniques, but appear to be well suited for dealing with detection problems as they allow for a simple way to estimate and control the percentage of false negatives by appropriate tuning of the confidence level.

We consider a setting in which there are enough positive examples to allow for reasonable estimates of 1-dimensional marginal probability distributions but no information is available on the negative examples. The underlying null hypothesis is the presence of a face in the image. The null distribution is unknown and estim   rom *positive training data*. Since no information is available on the alternative, the power of the test is boosted through multiple tests, selected during the training process with nonparametric independence tests. Each test is derived from an image measurement.

The learning process we present is efficient in the sense that increasing the number of training samples leads to better estimates of the underlying probability densities without increasing the computing cost at runtime.

4.1   Background

Traditional hypothesis tests rely on the basic assumption of knowing the probability distribution of the observable under the null hypothesis and a model for the alternative against which the test is run. Possibly the most common choice for an alternative is the shift model, effectively leading to one- or two-sided test such as, for example, the Student's one-sample t-test.

Here we estimate the null distribution $p(x)$ as the histogram of our measurements from the positive training data. We then define a probability density $f(t)$ as follows

$$\int_0^t f(z)dz = \int_{-\infty}^{+\infty} p(x)U_0(t - p(x))dx \qquad (6)$$

where $U_0(\cdot)$ is the unit step function. For a fixed $t \geq 0$, the integral on the l.h.s. is equal to the probability of the event

$$\mathsf{D}_t = p^{-1}([0,t]) \qquad (7)$$

(see the dashed area in Fig. 1). We then perform a one-sided test on $f(t)$ rejecting the null hypothesis for values of t lower than a critical value t_α. As usual, the significance level of the test is given by

$$\alpha = \int_0^{t^\alpha} f(t)dt.$$

Effectively, this test implements the maximum likelihood principle by rejecting the null hypothesis if the observable x falls in a region of small probability (see Fig. 1). Note that by Eqs. 6 and 7 the tail of f may account for disjoint intervals on the x-axis (see again Fig. 1).

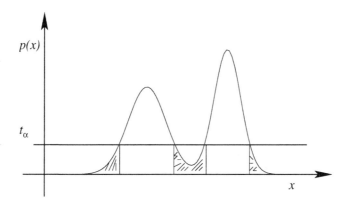

Fig. 1. The dashed areas of the distribution $p(x)$ contribute to the "tail" (or the reject region) $t \le t_\alpha$ of the distribution f defined by Eq. 6.

4.2   Outline of the Proposed Method

The proposed method is based on extracting a large number of features from images and estimate the probability distribution of each feature using the available positive training examples. A criterion derived from maximum likelihood is used to identify the most significant image features, then a rank test is performed to further select a maximal subset of pairwise independent features. Let N be the size of the set of features that survived the selections. At run time, a hypothesis test is performed for each of the N features. The null hypothesis is, in each case, the presence of a face. A face is detected if at least M of the N tests are passed. The significance of the global test depends on M as well as on the single tests.

The system can be summarized in four steps: *(i)* feature extraction, *(ii)* selection of salient features, *(iii)* selection of independent features, and *(iv)* testing against the object presence in the image. In the training phase, all steps are performed, while at runtime, after the features selected in the third stage have been computed, only the fourth step needs to be performed. We now describe each step in some detail considering the problem of face detection as a case study. The training set is the set of positive examples from the CBCL-MIT database (2429 images of size 19×19).

Feature Extraction During the first step we aim at computing a large number of potentially representative image measurements, with no limits on their type and number. In this section we list the image measurements based on raw pixels and ranks that we adopted. The current collection of image measurements is not exhaustive and can easily be enriched; we simply regard it as a starting point for validating our method.

For each image patch of size 19×19 (the size of the whole image in the training stage) we compute the following collection of features:

- Pixel gray values. We consider 19×19=361 grey values, one for each pixel.
- Integral measurements computed along specific directions (at the moment limited to vertical, horizontal, and 45° diagonal). These can be viewed as a subset of the Radon transform of the image, *i.e.* as a *tomographic* scan of the grey value image, and for this reason we refer to them as tomographies. We compute 19 vertical, 19 horizontal, and 37 diagonal tomographies, for a total of 75.
- Ranklets, a family of orientation selective rank features designed in close analogy with Haar wavelets [27]. Whereas Haar wavelets are a set of filters that act linearly on the intensity values of the image, ranklets are defined in terms of the relative order of pixel intensities and are not affected by equalization procedures. We compute 5184 horizontal, 5184 vertical, 5184 diagonal ranklets, for a total of 15,552.

Overall this amounts to estimate about 16,000 features.

Feature Selection In the second step we select a subset of the computed features according to their saliency. Considering the type of hypothesis test based on the distribution f of Eq. 7, a quite natural definition of saliency can be given in terms of t_α. For the required significance level α, the image measurement with the distribution p leading to the largest t_α has maximum saliency because no measurement falling in the accept region has probability smaller than t_α (see Fig. 1). An approximate implementation of the above criterion can be obtained by ranking the computed features according to the ratio r between the variance estimated from the histogram obtained with the training set and their natural definition interval ($[0, 255]$ for grey values and tomographies and $[-1, 1]$ for ranklets). Given a threshold $0 < \tau_1 < 1$, the features for which $r \leq \tau_1$ are retained while all the other features are discarded. This ensures that all the distributions of the selected features for the problem at hand are sufficiently peaked. Through this step with $\tau_1 = 0.15$, all single pixel measurements are discarded and the number of features reduced to about 2000.

The third step aims at selecting a subset of independent features out of the salient features identified in the second step. The reason for this is to reduce the number of features without compromising the power of the final test. This should ensure a faster rejection of the null hypothesis (the object is in the image) after a smaller number of tests. The selection is performed first running the Spearman's independence test [15] on all pairs of features of the same category. For each feature category Spearman's test is used to build a graph with as many nodes as features in the category. Given a threshold $0 < \tau_2 < 1$, an edge between two nodes is created if the corresponding features reject the independence hypothesis with probability lower than τ_2. Finally, maximally complete subgraphs — or *cliques* — are searched in each graph. For each graph, the clique nodes correspond to features pairwise independent with confidence greater than $1 - \tau_2$. With $\tau_2 = 0.5$ in our face detection problem we are left with 44 vertical ranklets, 64 horizontal ranklets, 329 diagonal ranklets, and 38 tomographies for a total of 475 features. The independence hypothesis is consistent with the posterior observation that features of the same clique correspond to not overlapping image regions.

Detection The fourth and final step tests the hypothesis of the presence of a face in the image. In the present setting, all images are 19×19 pixels and the hypothesis is simply whether, or not, an image is a face image. In this step the idea is to gather evidence for rejecting the null hypothesis – that is, that the image is a face image – by running all the tests, one for each of the selected, independent features.

It is interesting to see what happens if these tests are run on the training images. Fig. 2 shows the histogram of the number of tests passed with a certain confidence level $1 - \alpha$ for the training images with $\alpha = 0.2$. From Fig. 2 it is apparent that running sufficiently many tests, even with a very high confidence level for each single test, almost no positive example passes all tests (see the rightmost bins of Fig. 2). However, from each histogram, we can empirically estimate the number of tests to be passed to obtain any *overall* confidence level. Fig. 2 shows how to compute empirically the number of tests to be passed to achieve a given confidence level: the vertical lines drawn indicate an overall significance 0.05 (left) and 0.1 (right).

4.3   Experimental Results

We tested our system on the test sets of the MIT-CBCL database, that consists of 472 faces and 23'573 non-faces of size 19 × 19. We first ran experiments using features from one category only. The fraction M of tests to be passed for detecting a face is determined by looking at histograms similar to those of Fig. 2. The results, not reported here, show that the discriminating power of each category is not sufficient to reach a good characterization of faces. In particular, the diagonal ranklets, though sharply peaked across the training set, have almost zero discriminating power. For this reason we decided to discard them and use the remaining N=146 features. Using this reduced set of features we re-estimated the fraction of tests to be passed, obtaining M=110 for $\alpha = 0.1$.

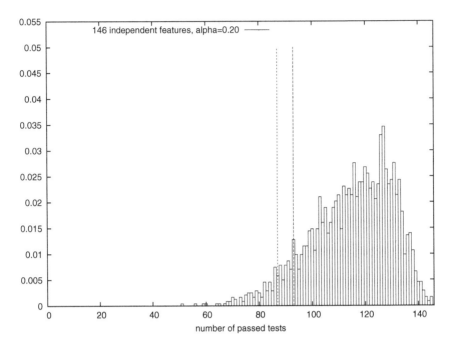

Fig. 2. Histogram of the number of tests passed by each training image ($\alpha = 0.2$ for all tests). The leftmost and rightmost vertical lines mark the overall significance level of 0.05 and 0.1 respectively.

The ROC in Fig. 3, obtained varying the significance of the single test, shows the overall results. The best performance is obtained by using the 146 featurs selected according to the proposed method. The use of 146 features randomly sampled or of 146 features with overlapping image support leads to inferior performances (see Fig. 3). The advantage of including ranklets in the feature set can be appreciated by looking the the ROC curve which is obtained using tomographies only. Only with ranklets the equal error rate is in line with the state-of-the-art on this database for whole face approaches [2, 27]. The performance of the described system is almost indistiguishable from a linear one-class SVM [28] trained on the same 146 features. In this work, the thresholds used to select peaked and pairwise independent image measurements were set empirically ($\tau_1 = 0.15$ and $\tau_2 = 0.5$, respectively). We are currently studying the effects of changing these parameters and the developing a technique for parameter estimation. Preliminary results on the use of the proposed method for finding faces in full size images are very promising (see Fig. 4 for results in face detection and Fig. 5 for face close-ups retrieved by our system). A prototype version, limited to the case of close-up, can be tested on our webpage: http://slipguru.disi.unige.it/research.

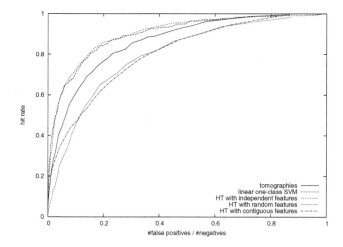

Fig. 3. ROC curves on the MIT-CBCL test set. The top curves are obtained using the 146 features selected by the proposed method and a one-class SVM trained on the same representation. The two lower curves are obtained using 146 randomly sampled and 146 contiguous features respectively, the middle curve with tomographies only (no ranklets).

Fig. 4. Some experimental results on face detection obtained with our system. The detected faces, are marked by a white frame at the detection scale.

Fig. 5. Some experimental results obtained with our system for face close-ups retrieval. The detected face, if any, is marked by a white frame at a certain scale.

We believe that the main merit of this approach lies in the direct application of simple, nonparametric statistical techniques with minimal assumptions on the probability distributions of the data. Clear strengths of this method are its generality, modularity, and wide applicability. On the other side, the flexibility of the approach can lead to suboptimal solutions unless some problem specific knowledge is injected into the system. Another interesting feature of this method is the limited computational cost, especially at run time. The tests, even if multiple, are very fast, making this system suitable for efficient multiscale search (on this respect, we obtained promising preliminary results, both for efficiency and detection precision).

Acknowledgments

We thank Fabrizio Smeraldi for many useful discussions and also for the idea, the code and the support on Ranklets. This work has been partially supported by the INFM Advanced Research Project MAIA, the FIRB Project ASTA RBAU01877P, the EU NoE Pascal (Pattern Analysis, Statistical Modelling and Computational Learning).

References

[1] N. Alon, S. Ben-David, N. Cesa-Bianchi, and D. Haussler. Scale-sensitive dimensions, uniform convergence, and learnability,. In *Symposium on Foundations of Computer Science*, 1993.

[2] M. Alvira and R. Rifkin. An empirical comparison of SNoW and SVMs for face detection. Technical Report AI Memo 2001-004 - CBCL Memo 193, MIT, January 2001.

[3] R. Chellappa, C. L. Wilson, and S. Sirohey. Human and machine recognition of faces: a survey. *Proc. IEEE*, 83(5):705–740, 1995.

[4] C. Cortes and V. Vapnik. Support vector networks. *Machine Learning*, 20:1–25, 1995.

[5] N. Cristianini and J. Shawe-Taylor. *An introduction to support vector machines (and other kernel based learning methods.* Cambridge University Press, 2000.

[6] F. Cucker and S. Smale. On the mathematical foundations of learning,. *Bull Am Math Soc*, 2001.

[7] L. Devroye, L. Györfi, and G. Lugosi. *A Probabilistic Theory of Pattern Recognition*. Springer, New York, 1996.

[8] T. Evgeniou, M. Pontil, and T. Poggio. Regularization networks and support vector machines,. *Advances in Computational Mathematics*, 13:1–50, 2000.

[9] F. Girosi, M. Jones, and T. Poggio. Regularization theory and neural networks architectures. *Neural Computation*, 7:219–269, 1995.

[10] T. Hastie, R. Tibshirani, and J. Friedman. *The elements of statistical learning. Data mining, inference, and prediction.* Springer Series in Statistics. Springer-Verlag, 2001.

[11] B. Heisele, T. Serre, M. Pontil, and T. Poggio. Component-based face detection. In *Proc. IEEE Conf. CVPR*, 2001.

[12] B. Heisele, T. Serre, M. Pontil, and T. Poggio. Component-based face detection. In *Proceedings of the IEEE Conference on Computer Vision and Pattern Recognition*, pages 657–662, 2001.

[13] E. Hjelmas and B. K. Low. Face detection: a survey. *Computer Vision and Image Understanding*, 83:236–274, 2001.

[14] M. Kearns and R. Shapire. Efficient distribution-free learning of probabilistic concepts. *Journal of Computer and Systems Sciences*, 48, 1994.

[15] E. L. Lehmann. *Nonparametrics: Statistical methods based on ranks.* Holden-Day, 1975.

[16] T. K. Leung, M. C. Burl, and P. Perona. Finding faces in cluttered scenes using random labeled graph matching. In *Proc. IEEE ICCV*, 1995.

[17] S. Z. Li, L. Zhu, Z.Q. Zhang, A. Blake, HJ Zhang, and H. Shum. statistical learning of multiview face detection. In *Proc. of the European Conference on Computer Vision*, 2002.

[18] A. Mohan, C. Papageorgiou, and T. Poggio. Example-based object detection in images by components. *IEEE Transactions on PAMI*, 23(4), 2001.

[19] E. Osuna, R. Freund, and F. Girosi. An improved training algorithm for support vector machines. In *IEEE Workshop on Neural Networks and Signal Processing*, 1997.

[20] E. Osuna, R. Freund, and F. Girosi. Training Support Vector Machines: an lication to face detection. In *Proc of CVPR*, 1997.

[21] C. Papageorgiou and T. Poggio. A trainable system for object detection. *natonal Journal of Computer Vision*, 38(1):15–33, 2000.

[22] J.C. Platt. Sequential minimal imization: A fast algorithm for training support vector machines. Technical Report MST-TR-98-14, Microsoft Research,, 1998.

[23] T.D. Rikert, M.J. Jones, and P. Viola. A cluster-based statistical model for object detection,. In *Proc. IEEE Conference on Computer Vision and Pattern Recognition*, 1999.

[24] H. Rowley, S. Baluja, and T. Kanade. Neural network-based face detection. *IEEE Trans. PAMI*, 20:23–38, 1998.

[25] H. Rowley, S. Baluja, and T. Kanade. rotation invariant neural network based face detection. In *Proc IEEE conf on Computer Vision and Pattern Recognition*, 1998.

[26] H. Schneiderman and T. Kanade. A statistical method for 3d object detection applied to faces and cars. In *Proc. IEEE Int Conf. CVPR*, 2000.

[27] F. Smeraldi. Ranklets: orientation selective non-parametric features applied to face detection. In *Proc. of the 16th ICPR, Quebec QC*, August 2002.

[28] D. Tax and R. Duin. Data domain description by support vectors. In M. Verleysen, editor, *ANN99*, pages 251–256. D. Facto Press, 1999.

[29] M. Turk and A. Pentland. eigenfaces for face recognition. *J. on Cognitive Neu-*, 3(1), 1991.

[30] V. Vapnik. *The nature of Statistical learning theory*. Springer, 1998.

[31] V. Vapnik. *Statistical learning theory*. John Wiley and sons, New York, 1998.

[32] V. Vapnik and A. Y. Chervonenkis. On the uniform convergence of relative frequencies of events to their probabilities,. *Th. Prob. and its Applications*, 17:264–280, 1971.

[33] P. Viola and M. Jones. Robust real-time object detection. In *II Int. Workshop on Stat. and Computat. Theories of vision - modeling, learning, computing and sampling*, 2001.

[34] G. Wahba. Splines models for observational data. *Series in Applied Mathematics*, 5, 1990.

[35] L. Wiskott, J.-M. Fellous, N. Krüger, and C. von der Malsburg. A statistical method for 3-d object detection applied to faces and cars. In *Proc. IEEE Int. Conf. on Image Processing*, 1997.

[36] M. Yang, D. J. Kriegman, and N. Ahuja. Detecting faces in images: a survey. *IEEE Trans on Pattern Analysis and Machine Intelligence*, 24(1), 2002.

Hand Detection by Direct Convexity Estimation

Dganit Maimon and Yehezkel Yeshurun

School of Computer Science
Tel Aviv University

Abstract. We suggest a novel attentional mechanism for detection of smooth convex and concave objects based on direct processing of intensity values. The operator detects the region of the forearm in images, enabling location of the hand. The operator is robust to variation in illumination, scale, pose, and hand orientation. This method uses the geometrical structure of the forearm, which is common to all people; therefore no limitation of the hand pose and no personal adjustments are required.

1. Introduction

Using motion against a static background is so far the most common attentional mechanism for hands (see [2],[3]). Using skin color is also a very widely used attentional mechanism (see [4],[5],[6]), and some recent work is based on shape and edge statistics (see [7],[8]). Though the methods above have many advantages, they suffer from severe limitations such as a strong influence from surrounding objects, limiting the system robustness, and sometimes pre-processing is required for the hand or for its surrounding area. We overcome these problems by means of a novel attentional operator that detects smooth three-dimensional convex or concave objects in the image. The operator is environment-neutral; is robust for hand pose and orientation, scaling, and illumination; and is capable of detecting the subject against a strongly textured background. It is employed for hand detection, specifically to detect the forearm, which is narrower end is connected to the hand. The operator answers the above problems, it requires a relatively short running time, and its robustness leads to reliable results. The actual hand boundaries are located using edge information.

2. Attentional Operator for Detection of Convex Regions

This section defines the attentional mechanism for convex and concave objects. The method takes advantage of the forearm's geometrical structure as a truncated cone.

2.1. Defining the Argument of Gradient

Let us estimate the gradient map of image $I(x; y)$ by: $\Delta I(x,y) \approx ([D_\sigma(x)G_\sigma(y)*I(x,y), G_\sigma(x)D_\sigma(y)*I(x,y)]$, where $G_\sigma(t)$ is the one-dimensional Gaussian with zero mean and standard deviation σ, and $D_\sigma(t)$ is the derivative of that Gaussian. We turn the

M. Tistarelli, J. Bigun, and E. Grosso (Eds.): Biometrics School 2003, LNCS 3161, pp. 105-113, 2005
© Springer-Verlag Berlin Heidelberg 2005

Cartesian representation of the intensity gradient into a polar representation. The argument (also denoted "phase", and usually marked by θ(x,y)), is defined by:

$$\theta(x, y) = \arg(\nabla I(x, y)) = \arctan(\frac{\partial}{\partial y} I(x, y), \frac{\partial}{\partial x} I(x, y))$$

where the two-dimensional arctangent is defined by:

$$\arctan(x, y) = \begin{cases} \arctan\left(\dfrac{y}{x}\right) & \text{if } x \geq 0 \\[2mm] \arctan\left(\dfrac{y}{x}\right) + \pi & \text{if } x < 0 \text{ and } y \geq 0 \\[2mm] \arctan\left(\dfrac{y}{x}\right) - \pi & \text{if } x < 0 \text{ and } y < 0 \end{cases}$$

and the one dimensional arctan(t) denotes the inverse function of tan(t) so that: $\arctan(t) : [-\infty, \infty] \mapsto [-\pi/2, \pi/2]$. The attentional mechanism is simply the derivative of the argument map with respect to the y direction:

$$\frac{\partial}{\partial y} \theta(x, y) \approx [G_\sigma(x) D_\sigma(y)] * \theta(x, y)$$

We denote $\dfrac{\partial}{\partial y} \theta(x, y)$ as Y-Phase.

2.2. Mathematical Formulation of Y-Phase Reaction to Cylinder

The projection of concave and convex objects can be estimated by paraboloids that are like a cylinder in extreme asymmetry. The paraboloid model is represented ([1]). Our mathematical formulation refers to a general cylinder of the form: $f(x,y) = (ay-bx-c)^2$, where a,b,c are constants, at least one of a,b is not equal to zero, and ay=bx+c is the axis of the cylinder. The first-order derivatives of the cylinder are: dx=-2b(ay-bx-c), dy=2a(ay-bx-c). The gradient argument is therefore: θ(x,y)=arctan(-2b(ay-bx-c) ,2a(ay-bx-c)). However, when b≠0, θ(x,y) derivative exists in the whole plane, except for the ray: {(x,y) | ay=bx+c }. At this ray, θ(x,y) has a first-order discontinuity so its derivative in any direction different from the cylinder axis tends to infinity on this ray. The fact that for a horizontal cylinder the derivative in the y direction at the ray of the y=c/a, while continuous at the rest of the plane, can be clearly seen in Fig. 1(c). Working in a discrete environment, the difference between two neighboring points from different sides of the axis is proportional to b/a, and the operator reaction is proportional to the axis slant so that horizontal cylinders are emphasized most. For vertical cylinders b=0 and θ(x,y)=arctan(0, a(y-c)) is constant and derivable anywhere in the plane.

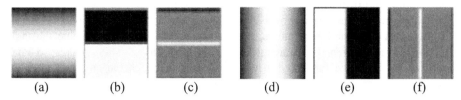

Fig. 1.   (a) The cylinder gray levels $I(x,y)=k(y-80)^2$.

(b) The argument of the gradient of (a). The discontinuity along the x-axis.

(c) Derivative of (b) in the y direction

(d) The cylinder gray levels $I(x,y)=k(x-80)^2$.

(e) The argument of the gradient of (d). The discontinuity along the x-axis.

(f) Derivative of (e) in the y direction

2.3. α-Phase: Extending to Any Direction

We also define the α-directional variant of Y-Phase, whose reaction to a cylinder whose axis in the α direction is maximal, rather than merely the horizontal cylinders. We do it by rotating the gradient argument by:

$$\theta_\alpha(x,y) = \begin{cases} \theta(x,y) + (\alpha - \pi) & \text{if} \theta(x,y) + (\alpha - \pi) \le \pi \\ \theta(x,y) + (\alpha - \pi) - 2\pi & \text{if} \theta(x,y) + (\alpha - \pi) > \pi \end{cases}$$

So the ray of discontinuity of the Y-Phase is transformed to a ray-forming angle of α radians with the positive part of the x-axis. We then derive the rotated argument of the gradient in the direction: α-π/2 (or: α+π/2), to get the response to the ray discontinuity (see fig 1). The operator reaction is proportional to difference between the axis slant and α.

2.4. Features of α-Phase

The two-dimensional objects of constant albedo form a linear gray-level function and are usually of no interest (for example, walls). It can be easily shown that the α-Phase attentional mechanism has zero response to planar objects. In addition, it can be shown that the response of α-Phase to edges of planar objects is finite, and is therefore smaller than its response to horizontal cylinders, and it is easy to prove that α-Phase is linear-dependent on scale. Another advantage of α-Phase is that it is invariant under any derivable monotonically increasing (in the strong sense) transform of the gray level image. The practical meaning of the theorem is that α-Phase is invariant, for example, under linear transformations, positive powers (where f(x; y) > 0), logarithm, and exponent. α-Phase is also invariant under linear combinations (with positive coefficients) and compositions of these functions, since such combinations are also derivable and strongly monotonically increasing. The functions mentioned above and their combinations are common in image processing for lighting improvement. This implies that α-Phase is invariant under a large variety of lighting conditions. In view of α-Phase invariance, the suggested model is not only a gray-level detector for cylinders, but also a detector of any derivable (strongly) monotonically increasing transformation of cylinders. This makes α-Phase particularly attractive for usage in various scenes in which the environment is not known in advance.

3. Forearm Detection Using α-Phase

3.1. Approximation by Truncated Cone

One of the underlying ideas of the theoretical model is the estimation of the gray levels describing convex and concave objects, in our case the forearm, using a truncated cone. Figure 2 shows such a cone, in synthetic form, along with magnified forearms. The forearm gray levels are similar to those of a cone.

Synthetic truncated cone

Original image   Forearm zoom + rotation   α phase at 90°   phase zoom + rotation

Fig. 2. The forearm exhibits strong similarity to the artificial truncated cone's gray levels, each column being created by the function f=bg-cy2 where bg is a background constant and c is a normalization constant calculated for each iteration. The iterations proceed from left to right; and each iteration is narrower by 1.5% of the maximal width at the left end of the cone. A clear response of α-Phase at 90° along the forearm is observed. The α-Phase of the forearm strongly reacts along the forearm; this behavior resembles that of the Y-Phase of a horizontal cone.

3.2. Defining Horizontal and Vertical Phase

The α-Phase operator has a maximal reaction to objects that exhibit convexity in the direction of the derivative; therefore, at angles similar to the forearm's orientation, the angular operator has a strong response along the forearm's length. The hand could be at any orientation, and at the beginning its orientation is unknown. Figure 3 demonstrates that using the operator only in the vertical and horizontal directions is an economical and efficient solution. We define the V-Phase operator as the sum of the vertical components, where α = 90° and 270°. The H-Phase operator is defined as the sum of the horizontal components, where α = 0° and 180°. As expected, the operators gain very high response along the forearm; therefore we search for a prolonged area where the operator attains high values. Although neither of the separate operators V-Phase and H-Phase covers every angle, the combination covers all angles, with a wide overlap. We define the VH-Phase method as using the V-Phase and H-Phase operators.

3.3. Robustness

The method is robust both for the hand's properties and for changes in the surrounding environment. In addition to orientations as demonstrated in the previous section, we demonstrate robustness to tilt (fig 4), self-rotation (fig 5) and size (fig 6).

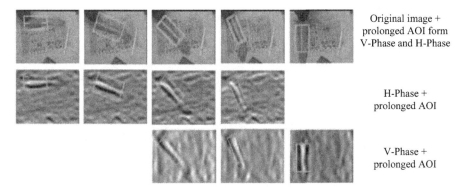

Original image +
prolonged AOI form
V-Phase and H-Phase

H-Phase +
prolonged AOI

V-Phase +
prolonged AOI

Fig. 3. Covering all forearms orientation. From top to bottom: the original image, the H-Phase and V-Phase. The forearm area attains very high response for at least one of the operators, with wide range of overlapping.

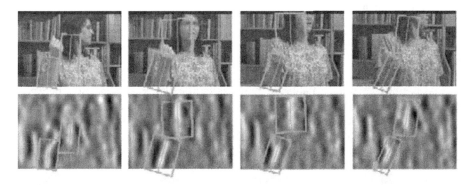

Fig. 4. Top row: a sequence of images where in each successive image the tilt is greater by approximately 22.5°; the covered range is almost 70°. Bottom row: V-Phase operator with AOI marked on it. In addition to the forearm, the hair receives high response from the operator. Using object dimension for edge map easily disqualifies the hair area.

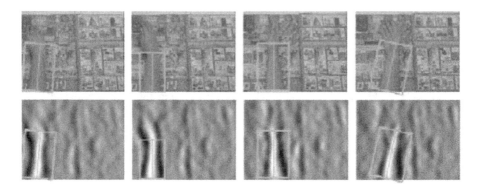

Fig. 5. At top, the original image with AOI marked on it. At bottom, the V-Phase image. Although the background is very cluttered, the forearm area gets very a high response of the V-Phase.

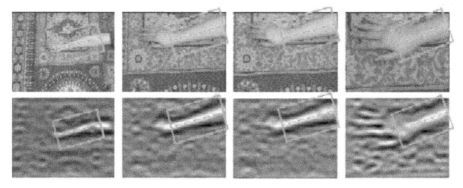

Fig. 6. At top, the original image with AOI marked on it. At bottom, the H-Phase image. The largest hand is more than 10 times larger than the smallest hand. The forearm area remains the dominant feature in the H-Phase maps.

4. Superiority of the VH-Phase Method

In this section we briefly delineate the result of extensive comparison between combination of H-Phase and V-Phase operators against the motion based method.

1. Reaction to 3D Objects: The VH-Phase method detects 3D objects, so both operators' (H-Phase and V-Phase) response to a hand made of cardboard with same external boundaries (2D object) is relatively low, as opposed to motion-based and color-based methods (fig 7).

2. Scaling-dependency: Color-based methods prefer large objects, whereas VH-Phase have linear dependency (fig 8).

3. The surrounding objects' color: VH-Phase operators use the surface area of the arm and therefore have very high response even when the background color is similar to the skin color, as opposed to motion-based and color -based methods where no color difference means no detection (fig 9)

4. Robust for illumination: Light intensity increases monotonically (in the strong sense), so the VH-Phase is not affected by lightning conditions, whereas other methods require optimal lightning conditions. Fig 10 has two images of the same scene, taken in different amount of lightning. The images include one factitious that is brighter then the real hand. The color base method succeed only when the lightning fits, when under lightning it focus on the factitious cardboard hand that become darker because of lacking light. The VH-Phase method ignore lightning amount correctly locates the real hand.

5. Conclusions

We introduce novel attentional operators (H-Phase and V-Phase) for detection of regions emanating from smooth convex or concave three-dimensional objects. We use it to detect the forearm, whence the hand. The operators are proved invariant under any derivable (strongly) monotonically increasing transformation of the image gray levels, which in practice means robustness to illumination changes. Robustness to orientation and scale is also demonstrated. The method is based on the geometrical structure of the forearm, which is common to all people; therefore no training stage is required. Furthermore, it uses only the surface area of the forearm and is not affected by the environment like motion-based and color -based method and thus remains free of their flaws.

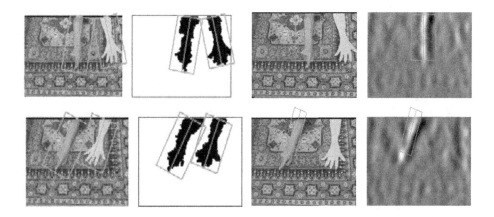

Fig. 7. Real hand vs. hand made of cardboard: We took two images from a sequence where both an artificial hand and a real hand are in motion. The motion -based method detects both real and artificial hands; VH-Phase detects only the real hand.

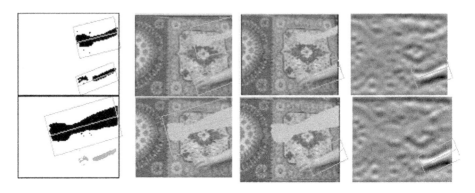

Fig. 8. Real hand vs. hand made of cardboard: The color-based method detects the largest object, or both when the sizes are similar. VH-Phase detects only the real hand, ignoring flat objects.

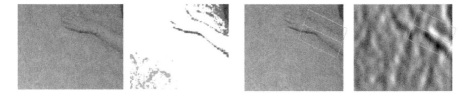

Fig. 9. The background is similar to the skin color. The color-based method fails by marking most of the area as AOI (all the white area); VH-Phase detects only the small area around the forearm.

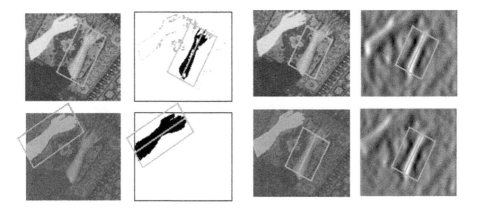

Fig. 10. Two images of the same scene, taken in different amount of lightning. The images include one factitious that is brighter then the real hand. The color base method succeed only when the lightning fits, when under lightning it focus on the factitious cardboard hand that become darker because of lacking light. The VH-Phase method ignore lightning amount correctly locates the real hand.

References

[1] A. Tankus, H. Yeshurun. Face detection by Direct Convexity Estimation. Pattern recognition letters.

[2] Kahn, Roger E, Swing M.J., Prokopowicz, P.N., and Firby R. James Gesture Recognition Using Perseus Architecture CVPR96 (734-741).

[3] Y. Cui and J. Weng, Hand segmentation using learning-based prediction and verification for hand sign recognition, in Proc. IEEE Conference on Computer Vision and Pattern Recognition, San Francisco, CA, pp. 88-93, June, 1996.

[4] Enno Littman and Helge Ritter "Adaptive Color Segmentation of Neural and Statistical Methods" TNN(8) 1, January 1997, pp. 175-185.

[5] Delamarre, Q. Faugeras, O.D., Finding Pose of Hand in Video Images: A Stereo-Based Approach, AFGR98

[6] Heap A.J., Real-Time Hand Tracking and Gesture Recognition using Smart Snakes, Proc. Interface to Real and Virtual Worlds, Montpellier, June 1995

[7] MacCormick, J.P, Isard, M., Partitioned Sampling, Articulated Objects, and Interface-Quality Hand Tracking, ECCV00.

[8] Sullivan, J. Blake, A. Isard, M. MacCormick, J.P. Object Localization by Bayesian Correlation, ICCV99 (1068-1075).

Template-Based Hand Detection and Tracking

R. Cipolla[1], B. Stenger[1], A. Thayananthan[1], and P.H.S. Torr[2]

[1] University of Cambridge, Department of Engineering, Trumpington Street, Cambridge, CB2 1PZ, UK
[2] Microsoft Research Ltd., 7 J J Thomson Ave, Cambridge CB3 0FB, UK

Abstract. Within this paper a technique for model-based 3D hand tracking is presented. A hand model is built from a set of truncated quadrics, approximating the anatomy of a real hand with few parameters. Given that the projection of a quadric onto the image plane is a conic, the contours can be generated efficiently. These model contours are used as shape templates to evaluate possible matches in the current frame. The evaluation is done within a hierarchical Bayesian filtering framework, where the posterior distribution is computed efficiently using a tree of templates. We demonstrate the effectiveness of the technique by using it for tracking 3D articulated and non-rigid hand motion from monocular video sequences in front of a cluttered background.

1   Introduction

Hand tracking has great potential as a tool for better human-computer interaction. Tracking hands, in particular articulated finger motion, is a challenging problem because the motion exhibits many degrees of freedom (DOF). Representing the hand pose by joint angles, the configuration space is 27 dimensional, 21 DOF for the joint angles and 6 for orientation and location. Given a kinematic hand model, one may attempt to use inverse kinematics to calculate the joint angles [19], however this problem is ill-posed when using a single view. It also requires exact feature localization, which is particularly difficult in the case of self-occlusion.

Most successful methods have followed the approach of using a geometric hand model, introduced by Rehg and Kanade [13] in the *DigitEyes* tracking system. Their hand model is constructed from truncated cylinders. The axes of these cylinders are projected into the image, and the distances to local edges are minimised using nonlinear optimisation. Heap and Hogg [9] use a deformable surface mesh model, which is constructed via principal component analysis (PCA) from example shapes obtained with an MRI scanner. This is essentially a 3D version of active shape models, and shape variation is captured by only a few principal components. The motion is not based on a physical deformation model and thus implausible finger motions can result. Wu *et al.* [20] model the articulated hand motion from data captured using a data glove. The tracker is based on importance sampling, and hypotheses are generated by projecting a 'cardboard model' into the image. This model is constructed from planar patches, and thus the system is view-dependent.

It is clear that the performance of a model-based tracker depends on the type of the used model. However, there is a trade-off between accurate modelling, and efficient rendering and comparison with the image data. In fact this is generally true when

M. Tistarelli, J. Bigun, and E. Grosso (Eds.): Biometrics School 2003, LNCS 3161, pp. 114–125, 2005.

modelling articulated objects for tracking, which is commonly done in the context of human body tracking (see [11] for a survey). A number of different models have been suggested in this context, using various primitives such as boxes, cylinders, ellipsoids or super-quadrics.

The next section describes the geometric hand model used in this paper. Section 3 reviews work on tree-based detection. A short introduction to Bayesian filtering is given in 4, and in section 5 we introduce filtering using a tree-based estimator. Tracking results on video sequences of hand motion are shown in section 6.

2   Modelling Hand Geometry

This section describes the construction of a hand model from truncated quadrics. The advantage of this method is that the object surface can be approximated with low complexity and that contours can be generated using tools from projective geometry. This hand model has previously been described in [15] but here it is used in a different tracking framework.

2.1   Projective Geometry of Quadrics and Conics

A quadric is a second degree implicit surface in 3D space, and it can be represented in homogeneous coordinates by a symmetric 4×4 matrix $\mathbf{Q}$ [8]. The surface is defined by all points $\mathbf{X} = [x, y, z, 1]^{\mathrm{T}}$ satisfying the equation

$$\mathbf{X}^{\mathrm{T}}\mathbf{Q}\mathbf{X} = 0. \tag{1}$$

Different families of quadrics are obtained from matrices $\mathbf{Q}$ of different ranks. Particular cases of interest are:

ellipsoids, represented by matrices $\mathbf{Q}$ with full rank;
cones and cylinders, represented by matrices $\mathbf{Q}$ with $\mathrm{rank}(\mathbf{Q}) = 3$;
a pair of planes π_0 and π_1, represented as $\mathbf{Q} = \pi_0 \pi_1^{\mathrm{T}} + \pi_1 \pi_0^{\mathrm{T}}$ with $\mathrm{rank}(\mathbf{Q}) = 2$.

Note that there are several other projective types of quadrics, such as hyperboloids or paraboloids, which like ellipsoids have a matrix of full rank. Under a Euclidean transformation $\mathbf{T} = \begin{bmatrix} \mathbf{R} & \mathbf{t} \\ \mathbf{0}^{\mathrm{T}} & 1 \end{bmatrix}$ the shape of a quadric is preserved, but in the new coordinate system $\mathbf{Q}$ is represented by $\hat{\mathbf{Q}} = \mathbf{T}^{-\mathrm{T}}\mathbf{Q}\mathbf{T}^{-1}$.

A quadric has nine degrees of freedom, corresponding to the independent elements of $\mathbf{Q}$ up to a scale factor. Given a number of point correspondences or outlines in multiple views, quadric surfaces can be reconstructed, as shown by Cross and Zisserman [6]. It is also suggested that for many objects using a piecewise quadric representation gives an accurate and compact surface representation. In order to employ quadrics for modelling such general shapes, it is necessary to truncate them. For any quadric $\mathbf{Q}$ the truncated quadric $\mathbf{Q}_{\Pi}$ can be obtained by finding points $\mathbf{X}$ satisfying:

$$\mathbf{X}^{\mathrm{T}}\mathbf{Q}\mathbf{X} = 0 \quad \text{and} \quad \mathbf{X}^{\mathrm{T}}\mathbf{\Pi}\mathbf{X} \geq 0, \tag{2}$$

where Π is a matrix representing a pair of clipping planes (see figure 1a). The image of a quadric $\mathbf{Q} = \begin{bmatrix} \mathbf{A} & \mathbf{b} \\ \mathbf{b}^T & c \end{bmatrix}$ seen from a normalised projective camera $\tilde{\mathbf{P}} = [\mathbb{I} \mid \mathbf{0}]$ is a conic $\mathbf{C}$ given by

$$\mathbf{C} = c\mathbf{A} - \mathbf{b}\mathbf{b}^T, \tag{3}$$

as shown in figure 1b. In order to obtain the image of a quadric $\mathbf{Q}$ in an arbitrary projective camera $\mathbf{P}$ it is necessary to compute the transformation $\mathbf{H}$ such that $\mathbf{PH} = [\mathbb{I} \mid \mathbf{0}]$. This normalising transformation is given by the matrix $\mathbf{H} = [\mathbf{P}^\dagger | \mathbf{p}^\perp]$, where $\mathbf{P}^\dagger$ is the pseudo inverse of $\mathbf{P}$ and $\mathbf{p}^\perp$ is the camera centre or the null vector of $\mathbf{P}$ (see [5]).

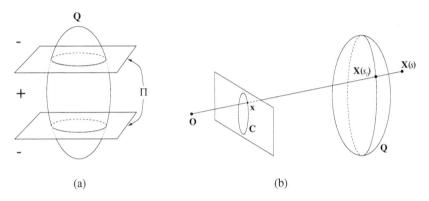

(a)   (b)

Fig. 1. Projection of a quadric. *(a) A truncated quadric* $\mathbf{Q}_\Pi$*, here a truncated ellipsoid, can be obtained by finding points on quadric* $\mathbf{Q}$ *which satisfy* $\mathbf{X}^T \Pi \mathbf{X} \geq 0$*. (b) The projection of a quadric* $\mathbf{Q}$ *into the image plane is a conic* $\mathbf{C}$*.*

2.2   Description of the Hand Model

The hand model is built using a set of quadrics $\{\mathbf{Q}_i\}_{i=1}^q$, representing the anatomy of a human hand as shown in figure 2. We use a hierarchical model with 27 degrees of freedom (DOF): 6 for the global hand position, 4 for the pose of each finger and 5 for the pose of the thumb. Starting from the palm and ending at the tips, the coordinate system of each quadric is defined relative to the previous one in the hierarchy. The palm is modelled using a truncated cylinder, its top closed by a half-ellipsoid. Each finger consists of three segments of a cone, one for each phalanx. They are connected by hemispheres, representing the joints. A default shape is first obtained by taking measurements from a real hand. Given the image data, shape matching can be used to estimate a set of shape parameters, including finger lengths and a width parameter [17].

2.3   Generation of the Contours

Each clipped quadric of the hand model is projected individually as described in section 2.1, generating a list of clipped conics. For each conic matrix $\mathbf{C}$ we use eigendecomposition to obtain a factorisation given by

$$\mathbf{C} = \mathbf{T}^{-T}\mathbf{D}\mathbf{T}^{-1}. \tag{4}$$

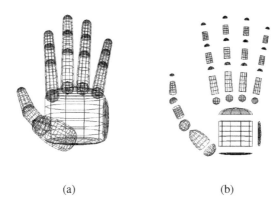

(a)   (b)

Fig. 2. Geometric hand model. *The hand model has 27 degrees of freedom is constructed using truncated quadrics as building blocks. Depicted is (a) a front view and (b) an exploded view.*

The diagonal matrix $\mathbf{D}$ represents a conic aligned with the x- and y-axis and centred at the origin. The matrix $\mathbf{T}$ is the Euclidean transformation that maps this conic onto $\mathbf{C}$. We can therefore draw $\mathbf{C}$ by drawing $\mathbf{D}$ and transforming the points according to $\mathbf{T}$. The drawing of $\mathbf{D}$ is carried out by different methods, depending on its rank. For $\text{rank}(\mathbf{D}) = 3$ we draw an ellipse, for $\text{rank}(\mathbf{D}) = 2$ we draw a pair of lines.

The next step is occlusion handling. Consider a point $\mathbf{x}$ on the conic $\mathbf{C}$, obtained by projecting the quadric $\mathbf{Q}$, as shown in figure 1. The camera centre and $\mathbf{x}$ define a 3D ray L. Each point $\mathbf{X} \in L$ is given by $\mathbf{X}(s) = \begin{bmatrix} \mathbf{x} \\ s \end{bmatrix}$, where s is a free parameter determining the depth of the point in space, such that the point $\mathbf{X}(0)$ is at infinity and $\mathbf{X}(\infty)$ is at the camera centre. The point of intersection of the ray with the quadric $\mathbf{Q}$ is found by solving the equation

$$\mathbf{X}(s)^{\mathrm{T}}\mathbf{Q}\mathbf{X}(s) = 0 \tag{5}$$

for s. Writing $\mathbf{Q} = \begin{bmatrix} \mathbf{A} & \mathbf{b} \\ \mathbf{b}^{\mathrm{T}} & c \end{bmatrix}$, the unique solution of (5) is given by $s_0 = -\mathbf{b}^{\mathrm{T}}\mathbf{x}/c$. In order to check if $\mathbf{X}(s_0)$ is visible, (5) is solved for each of the other quadrics $\mathbf{Q}_i$ of the hand-model. In the general case there are two solutions s_1^i and s_2^i, yielding the points where the ray intersects with quadric $\mathbf{Q}_i$. The point $\mathbf{X}(s_0)$ is visible if $s_0 \geq s_j^i \quad \forall i, j$, in which case the point $\mathbf{x}$ is drawn. Figure 3 shows examples of hand model projections.

2.4   Learning Natural Hand Articulation

Model-based trackers commonly use a 3D geometric model with an underlying biomechanical deformation model [1, 2, 13]. Each finger can be modelled as a kinematic chain with 4 DOF, and the thumb with 5 DOF. Thus articulated hand motion lies in a 21 dimensional joint angle space. However, hand motion is highly constrained as each joint can only move within certain limits. Furthermore the motion of different joints is correlated, for example, most people find it difficult to bend the little finger while keeping the ring finger fully extended at the same time. Thus hand articulation is expected to lie in a compact region within the 21 dimensional angle space. We used a data

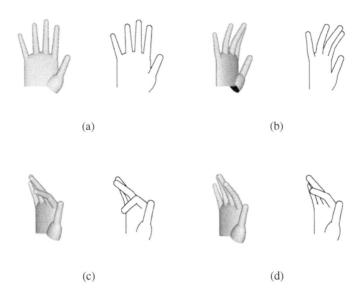

Fig. 3. Examples of model projections. *(a)-(d) show different hand poses. For each example the 3D hand model is shown on the left and its projection into the image plane on the right. Note that self-occlusion is handled when generating the contours.*

glove to collect a large number of joint angles in order to capture natural hand articulation. Experiments with 15 sets of joint angles captured from three different subjects, show that in all cases 95 percent of the variance is captured by the first eight principal components, in 10 cases within the first seven, which confirms the results reported by Wu   in [20]. Figure 4 shows trajectories projected onto the first three eigenvectors between a set of hand poses. As described in the next section, this lower dimensional eigen-space will be quantised into a set of discrete states. Hand motion is then modelled by a first order Markov process between these states. Given a large amount of training data, higher order models can be learned.

3   Tree-Based Detection

For real applications the problem of tracker initialisation, as well as the handling of self-occlusion and cluttered backgrounds remain obstacles. Current state-of-the-art systems often employ a version of particle filtering, allowing for multiple hypotheses. The use of particle filters is primarily motivated by the need to overcome ambiguous frames in a video sequence so that the tracker is able to recover. Another way to overcome the problem of losing lock is to treat tracking as object detection at each frame. Thus if the target is lost in one frame, this does not affect any subsequent frame. Template based methods have yielded good results for locating deformable objects in a scene with no prior knowledge, e.g. for hands or pedestrians [2, 7, 14, 17]. These methods are made robust and efficient by the use of distance transforms such as the chamfer or Haus-

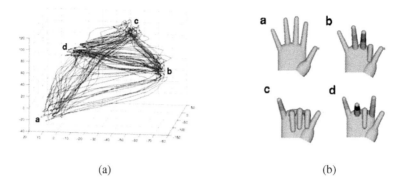

(a)   (b)

Fig. 4. Paths in the configuration space found by PCA. *(a) The figure shows a trajectory of projected hand state vectors onto the first three principal components. (b) The hand configurations corresponding to the four end points in (a).*

dorff distance between template and image [3, 10], which were originally developed for matching a single template. A key suggestion was that multiple templates could be dealt with efficiently by building a template hierarchy and a coarse-to-fine search [7, 12]. The idea is to group similar templates and represent them with a single prototype template together with an estimate of the variance of the error within the cluster, which is used to define a matching threshold. The prototype is first compared to the image; only if the error is below the threshold are the templates within the cluster compared to the image. This clustering is done at various levels, resulting in a hierarchy, with the templates at the leaf level covering the space of all possible templates.

If a parametric object model is available, another option to build the tree is by partitioning the state space. Each level of the tree defines a partition with increasing resolution, the leaves defining the finest partition. Such a tree is depicted schematically in figure 5(a), for a single rotation parameter. This tree representation has the advantage that prior information is encoded efficiently, as templates with large distance in parameter space are likely to be in different sub-trees.

It may be argued that there is no need for a parametric model and that an exemplar-based approach could be followed, as by Toyama and Blake in [18]. However, for models with many degrees of freedom the storage space for templates becomes excessive. The use of a parametric model allows the combination of an on-line and off-line approach in the tree-based algorithm. Once the leaf level is reached more child templates can be generated for further optimisation. Hierarchical detection works well for locating a hand in images, and yet often there are ambiguous situations that could be resolved by using temporal information. The next section describes the Bayesian framework for filtering.

4   Bayesian Filtering

Filtering is the problem of estimating the state (hidden variables) of a system given a history of observations. Define, at time t, the state parameter vector as θ_t, and the data

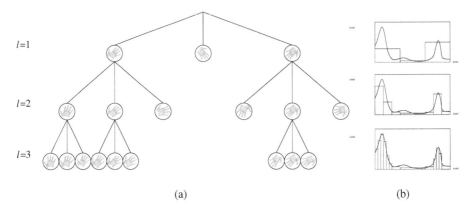

(a)   (b)

Fig. 5. Tree-based estimation of the posterior density. *(a) Associated with the nodes at each level is a non-overlapping set in the state space, defining a partition of the state space (here rotation angle). The posterior distribution for each node is evaluated using the centre of each set, depicted by a hand rotated by a specific angle. Sub-trees of nodes with low posterior probability are not further evaluated. (b) Corresponding posterior density (continuous) and the piecewise constant approximation using tree-based estimation. The modes of the distribution are approximated with higher precision at each level.*

(observations) as $\mathbf{D}_t$, with $\mathbf{D}_{1:t-1}$, being the set of data from time 1 to $t-1$; and the data $\mathbf{D}_t$ are conditionally independent at each time step given the $\boldsymbol{\theta}_t$. In our specific application $\boldsymbol{\theta}_t$ is the state of the hand (set of joint angles, location and orientation) and $\mathbf{D}_t$ is the image at time t (or some set of features extracted from that image). Thus at time t the posterior distribution of the state vector is given by the following recursive relation

$$\Pr(\boldsymbol{\theta}_t|\mathbf{D}_{1:t}) = \frac{\Pr(\mathbf{D}_t|\boldsymbol{\theta}_t)\Pr(\boldsymbol{\theta}_t|\mathbf{D}_{1:t-1})}{\Pr(\mathbf{D}_t|\mathbf{D}_{1:t-1})}, \tag{6}$$

where the normalising constant is

$$\Pr(\mathbf{D}_t|\mathbf{D}_{1:t-1}) = \int \Pr(\mathbf{D}_t|\boldsymbol{\theta}_t)\Pr(\boldsymbol{\theta}_t|\mathbf{D}_{1:t-1})d\boldsymbol{\theta}_t. \tag{7}$$

Th   rm $\Pr(\boldsymbol{\theta}_t|\mathbf{D}_{1:t-1})$ in (6) is obtained from the Chapman-Kolmogorov equation:

$$\Pr(\boldsymbol{\theta}_t|\mathbf{D}_{1:t-1}) = \int \Pr(\boldsymbol{\theta}_t|\boldsymbol{\theta}_{t-1})\Pr(\boldsymbol{\theta}_{t-1}|\mathbf{D}_{1:t-1})d\boldsymbol{\theta}_{t-1} \tag{8}$$

with the initial prior pdf $\Pr(\boldsymbol{\theta}_0|\mathbf{D}_0)$ assumed known. It can be seen that (6) and (8) both involve integrals. Except for certain simple distributions these integrals are in-tractable and so approximation methods must be used. As has been mentioned, Monte Carlo methods represent one way of evaluating these integrals. Alternatively, hierarchi-cal detection provides a very efficient way to evaluate the likelihood $\Pr(\mathbf{D}_t|\boldsymbol{\theta}_t)$ in a deterministic manner, even when the state space is high dimensional; as the number of templates in the tree increases exponentially with the number of levels in the tree. This leads us to consider dividing up the state space into non-overlapping sets, just as the templates in the tree cover the regions of parameter space. Typically this methodology has been applied using an evenly spaced grid and is thus exponentially expensive as the dimension of the state space increases. In this paper we combine the tracking process with the empirically successful process of tree-based detection as laid out in section 3 resulting in an efficient deterministic filter.

5 Filtering Using a Tree-Based Estimator

Our aim is to design an algorithm that can take advantage of the efficiency of the tree-based search whilst also yielding a good approximation to Bayesian filtering. We design a grid-based filter, in which a multi-resolution partition is provided by the tree as given in Section 3. Thus we will consider a grid defined by the leaves of the tree. Because the distribution is characterised by being almost zero in large regions of the state space with some isolated peaks, many of the grid regions can be discarded as possessing negligible probability mass. The tree-based search provides an efficient way to rapidly concentrate computation on significant regions. At the lowest level of the tree the posterior distribution will be assumed to be piecewise constant. This distribution will be mostly zero for many of the leaves. At each tree level the regions with high posterior are identified and explored in finer detail in the next level (Figure 5b). It is to be expected that the higher levels will not yield accurate approximations to the posterior. However, just as for the case of detection, the upper levels of the tree can be used to discard inadequate hypotheses, for which the negative log posterior of the set exceeds a threshold value. The thresholds at the higher levels of the tree are set conservatively so as to not discard good hypotheses too soon. The equations of Bayesian filtering (6)-(8), are recast to update these states. For more details see [16].

5.1 Formulating the Likelihood

A key ingredient for any tracker is the likelihood function $p(\mathbf{D}_t|\boldsymbol{\theta}_t)$, which relates the observations $\mathbf{D}_t$ to the unknown state $\boldsymbol{\theta}_t$. For hand tracking finding good features and a likelihood function is challenging, as there are few features which can be detected and tracked reliably. Colour values and edges contours appear to be suitable and have been used frequently in the past [2, 20]. Thus the data is taken to be composed of two sets of observations, those from edge data $\mathbf{D}_t^{edge}$ and from colour data $\mathbf{D}_t^{col}$. The likelihood function is assumed to factor as

$$p(\mathbf{D}_t|\boldsymbol{\theta}_t) = p(\mathbf{D}_t^{edge}|\boldsymbol{\theta}_t)\, p(\mathbf{D}_t^{col}|\boldsymbol{\theta}_t). \tag{9}$$

The likelihood term for edge contours $p(\mathbf{D}_t^{edge}|\boldsymbol{\theta}_t)$ is based on the chamfer distance function [3, 4]. Given the set of projected model contour points $\mathcal{U} = \{\mathbf{u}_i\}_{i=1}^n$ and the set of Canny edge points $\mathcal{V} = \{\mathbf{v}_j\}_{j=1}^m$, a quadratic chamfer distance function is given by

$$d_{cham}^2(\mathcal{U}, \mathcal{V}) = \frac{1}{n} \sum_{i=1}^n d^2(i, \mathcal{V}), \tag{10}$$

where $d(i, \mathcal{V}) = \max(\min_{v_j \in \mathcal{V}} ||u_i - v_j||, \tau)$ is the thresholded distance between the point, $u_i \in \mathcal{U}$, and its closest point in $\mathcal{V}$. Using a threshold value τ makes the matching more robust to outliers and missing edges. The chamfer distance between two shapes can be computed efficiently using a distance transform, where the template edge points are correlated with the distance transform of the image edge map. Edge orientation is included by computing the distance only for edges with similar orientation, in order to make the distance function more robust [12]. We also exploit the fact that part of an edge normal on the interior of the contour should be skin-coloured.

In constructing the colour likelihood function $p(\mathbf{D}_t^{col}|\boldsymbol{\theta}_t)$, we seek to explain all the image pixel data given the proposed state. Given a state, the pixels in the image $\mathcal{I}$ are partitioned into a set of object pixels $\mathcal{O}$, and a set of background pixels $\mathcal{B}$. Assuming pixel-wise independence, the likelihood can be factored as

$$p(\mathbf{D}_t^{col}|\boldsymbol{\theta}_t) = \prod_{k \in \mathcal{I}} p(I_t(k)|\boldsymbol{\theta}_t) = \prod_{o \in \mathcal{O}} p(I_t(o)|\boldsymbol{\theta}_t) \prod_{b \in \mathcal{B}} p(I_t(b)|\boldsymbol{\theta}_t), \qquad (11)$$

where $I_t(k)$ is the intensity normalised rg-colour vector at pixel location k at time t. The object colour distribution is modeled as a Gaussian distribution in the normalised colour space, and a uniform distribution is assumed for the background. For efficiency, we evaluate only the edge likelihood term while traversing the tree, and incorporate the colour likelihood only at the leaf level.

6   Results

We demonstrate the effectiveness of our technique by tracking both hand motion and finger articulation in cluttered scenes using a single camera. The results reveal the ability of the tree-structure to handle ambiguity arising from self-occlusion and 3D motion. In the first sequence (figure 6) we track the global 3D motion of a pointing hand. The 3D rotations are limited to a hemisphere. At the leaf level, the tree has the following resolutions: 15 degrees in two 3D rotations, 10 degrees in image rotation and 5 different scales. These 12,960 templates are then combined with a search at 2-pixel resolution in the image translation space. In the second example (figure 7) finger articulation is tracked while the hand is making transitions between different types of gestures. The tree is built by partitioning a lower dimensional eigen-space. Applying PCA to the data set shows that more than 96 percent of the variance is captured within the first four principal components, thus we partition the four dimensional eigen-space. The number of nodes at the leaf level in this case is 9,163. In the third sequence (figure 8) tracking is demonstrated for global hand motion together with finger articulation. The manifolds in section 2.4 are used to model the articulation. The articulation parameters for the thumb and fingers are approximated by the first 2 eigenvectors of the joint angle data set obtained from opening and closing of the hand. For this sequence the range of global hand motion is restricted to a smaller region, but it still has 6 DOF. In total 35,000 templates are used at the leaf level. The tree evaluation takes approximately 2 to 5 seconds per frame on a 1GHz Pentium IV machine. Note that in all cases the hand model was automatically initialised by searching the complete tree in the first frame of the sequence.

Fig. 6. Tracking a pointing hand in front of clutter.
projected contours superimposed (top) and corresponding 3D avatar models (bottom), which are estimated using our tree-based algorithm. The hand is translating and rotating. A 2D deformable template would have problems coping with topological shape changes caused by self-occlusion.

7 Summary and Conclusion

Within this paper we have described a model-based hand tracking system which overcomes some of the major obstacles which have limited the use of hand trackers in practical applications. These are the handling of self-occlusion, tracking in cluttered backgrounds, and tracker initialisation.

Our algorithm uses a tree of templates, generated from a 3D geometric hand model. The model is constructed from a set of truncated quadrics, and its contours can be projected into the image plane while handling self-occlusion. Articulated hand motion is learned from training data collected using a data glove. The likelihood cost function is based on the chamfer distance between projected contours and edges in the image. Additionally, edge orientation and skin colour information is used, making the matching more robust in cluttered backgrounds. The problem of tracker initialisation is solved by searching the tree in the first frame without the use of any prior information. We have tested the tracking method on a number of sequences including hand articulation and cluttered backgrounds. Furthermore within these sequences the hand undergoes rotations leading to significant topological changes in the projected contours. The tracker performs well even in these circumstances.

Acknowledgements The authors would like to thank the Gottlieb Daimler–and Karl Benz–Foundation, the EPSRC, the Gates Cambridge Trust, and the Overseas Research Scholarship Programme for their support.

References

[1] K. N. An, E. Y. Chao, W. P. Cooney, and R. L. Linscheid. Normative model of human hand for biomechanical analysis. *J. Biomechanics*, 12:775–788, 1979.

[2] V. Athitsos and S. Sclaroff. Estimating 3D hand pose from a cluttered image. In *Proc. Conf. Computer Vision and Pattern Recognition*, Madison, USA, June 2003. to appear.

[3] H. G. Barrow, J. M. Tenenbaum, R. C. Bolles, and H. C. Wolf. Parametric correspondence and chamfer matching: Two new techniques for image matching. In *Proc. 5th Int. Joint Conf. Artificial Intelligence*, pages 659–663, 1977.

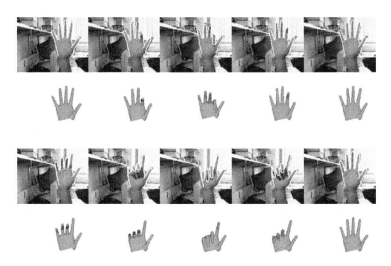

Fig. 7. Tracking finger articulation. *In this sequence a number of different finger motions are tracked. The images are shown with projected contours superimposed (top) and corresponding 3D avatar models (bottom), which are estimated using our tree-based filter. The nodes in the tree are found by hierarchical clustering of training data in the parameter space, and dynamic information is encoded as transition probabilities between the clusters.*

[4] G. Borgefors. Hierarchical chamfer matching: A parametric edge matching algorithm. *IEEE Trans. Pattern Analysis and Machine Intell.*, 10(6):849–865, November 1988.

[5] R. Cipolla and P. J. Giblin. *Visual Motion of Curves and Surfaces*. Cambridge University Press, Cambridge, UK, 1999.

[6] G. Cross and A. Zisserman. Quadric reconstruction from dual-space geometry. In *Proc. 6th Int. Conf. on Computer Vision*, pages 25–31, Bombay, India, January 1998.

[7] D. M. Gavrila. Pedestrian detection from a moving vehicle. In *Proc. 6th European Conf. on Computer Vision*, volume II, pages 37–49, Dublin, Ireland, June/July 2000.

[8] R. I. Hartley and A. Zisserman. *Multiple View Geometry in Computer Vision*. Cambridge University Press, Cambridge, UK, 2000.

[9] A. J. Heap and D. C. Hogg. Towards 3-D hand tracking using a deformable model. In *2nd International Face and Gesture Recognition Conference*, pages 140–145, Killington, USA, October 1996.

[10] D. P. Huttenlocher, J. J. Noh, and W. J. Rucklidge. Tracking non-rigid objects in complex scenes. In *Proc. 4th Int. Conf. on Computer Vision*, pages 93–101, Berlin, May 1993.

[11] T. B. Moeslund and E. Granum. A survey of computer vision-based human motion capture. *Computer Vision and Image Understanding*, 81(3):231–268, 2001.

[12] C. F. Olson and D. P. Huttenlocher. Automatic target recognition by matching oriented edge pixels. *Transactions on Image Processing*, 6(1):103–113, January 1997.

[13] J. M. Rehg. *Visual Analysis of High DOF Articulated Objects with Application to Hand Tracking*. PhD thesis, Carnegie Mellon University, Dept. of Electrical and Computer Engineering, 1995. TR CMU-CS-95-138.

Fig. 8. Tracking a hand opening and closing with rigid body motion. *This sequence is challenging because the hand undergoes translation and rotation while opening and closing the fingers. 6* DOF *for rigid body motion plus 2* DOF *using manifolds for finger flexion and extension are tracked successfully with our tree-based algorithm.*

[14] N. Shimada, K. Kimura, and Y. Shirai. Real-time 3-D hand posture estimation based on 2-D appearance retrieval using monocular camera. In *Proc. Int. WS. RATFG-RTS*, pages 23–30, Vancouver, Canada, July 2001.

ça, and R. Cipolla. Model based 3D tracking of an articulated hand. In *Proc. Conf. Computer Vision and Pattern Recognition*, volume II, pages 310–315, Kauai, USA, December 2001.

[16] B. Stenger, A. Thayananthan, P. H. S. Torr, and R. Cipolla. Hand tracking using a tree-based estimator. Technical Report CUED/F-INFENG/TR 456, University of Cambridge, Department of Engineering, 2003.

[17] A. Thayananthan, B. Stenger, P. H. S. Torr, and R. Cipolla. Shape context and chamfer matching in cluttered scenes. In *Proc. Conf. Computer Vision and Pattern Recognition*, Madison, USA, June 2003. to appear.

[18] K. Toyama and A. Blake. Probabilistic tracking with exemplars in a metric space. *Int. Journal of Computer Vision*, pages 9–19, June 2002.

[19] Y. Wu and T. S. Huang. Capturing articulated human hand motion: A divide-and-conquer approach. In *Proc. 7th Int. Conf. on Computer Vision*, volume I, pages 606–611, Corfu, Greece, September 1999.

[20] Y. Wu, J. Y. Lin, and T. S. Huang. Capturing natural hand articulation. In *Proc. 8th Int. Conf. on Computer Vision*, volume II, pages 426–432, Vancouver, Canada, July 2001.

3D Face Recognition Using Stereoscopic Vision

U. Castellani, M. Bicego, G. Iacono, and V. Murino

Dipartimento di Informatica, Università di Verona
Ca' Vignal 2, Strada Le Grazie 15
37134 Verona, Italia
{castellani,bicego,murino}@sci.univr.it

Abstract. In this paper a new complete system for 3D face recognition is presented. 3D face recognition presents several advantages against 2D face recognition, as, for example, invariance to illumination conditions. The proposed system makes use of a stereo methodology, that does not require any expensive range sensors. The 3D image of the face is modelled using Multilevel B-Splines coefficients, that are classified using Support Vector Machines. Preliminary experimental evaluation has produced encouraging results, making the proposed system a promising low cost 3D face recognition system.

1 Introduction

Face recognition is undoubtedly an interesting research area, growing in importance in recent years, due to its applicability as a biometric system in commercial and security applications. The face recognition system has the appealing characteristic of not being an invasive control tool, as compared with fingerprint or iris biometric systems.

The most typical approach to face recognition is to analyze 2D face images, and a large literature is available on this topic (for a review see [1], and [2]). The analysis of 2D face has some inherent drawbacks: for example it is not able to distinguish a real face from a picture of a face, since it does not consider depth information. This could represent an awkward problem, especially in the authentication context. Moreover, most part of techniques proposed in the literature suffers from illumination changes problems.

The analysis of 3D images of a face represents a possible solution for both these problems. Although 3D facial analysis has been already applied in some research areas, as compression and synthesis for videoconferencing [3], recognition of faces basing on range images is still weakly addressed in the literature [4,5,6,7,8,9]. More in detail, the first system that analyzes 3D faces was presented in [4]: the method identified facial features points, based on local curvature computed from range images. The face was segmented in convex and concave regions, and features were determined from these regions. No recognition was performed in this system. Gordon [5,6] was the first that realized a recognition system based on range data. He computed geometric features of the sensed surface, integrating some a priori knowledge. Recognition was performed using a template matching

M. Tistarelli, J. Bigun, and E. Grosso (Eds.): Biometrics School 2003, LNCS 3161, pp. 126–137, 2005.

approach and a classification system in the feature space. Another approach was proposed in [7,8], where the 3D information was determined using a coded light approach with two separate sensors. The classification step was performed using an eigenface approach and HMM-based technique. More recently, the same authors present another system [9], that classifies range images, acquired using a multi sensor system. The canonical position is determined from the range images face, and a 3D Haussdorff distance is used for the classification step.

In this paper a new complete system for 3D face recognition is proposed, based on stereoscopic images analysis. The process of stereo reconstruction aims at recovering the 3D structure from a pair of images by searching for *conjugate points*, i.e., points in the left and right images that are projections of the same scene point. The difference between the positions of conjugate points is called *disparity*. Stereo is a well known issue in Computer Vision, to which many articles have been devoted (see [10] for a survey). The system proposed in this paper has a clear advantage with respect to the previously introduced: the acquisition process is fast and entirely low cost. In fact, the 3D information are acquired using two cameras by applying the stereoscopic principles, without any need of particularly expensive range sensors. Furthermore, the stereo setup calibration is very easy and fast and there are different standard implemented methods freely available on the web. This aspect is really important, especially in the view of enlarging the applicability of the biometric technologies to real problems.

The range image obtained by the stereoscopic analysis is approximated using Multilevel B-Splines [11], an interpolation and approximation technique for scattered data. The resulting approximation coefficients were used as features for the classification, carried out by the Support Vector Machines (SVM) [12]. The reasons underlying the choice of using Multilevel B-Splines and Support Vector Machines are the following: from one hand, Multilevel B-Splines coefficients have been chosen for their approximation capabilities, able to manage slight changes in facial expression. On the other hand, even if a considerable dimensionality reduction is obtained by this technique with respect to considering the whole image [13], the resulting space is still large. Standard classifiers could be affected by the so called curse of dimensionality problem; SVMs, instead, are well suited to work in very high dimensional spaces (see for example [13]). This classification system has been already employed by the authors in the context of 2D face recognition [14]. In this version we explore the possibility to estimate the face surfaces directly from the 3D data obtained by the acquisition system.

The proposed system has been used to collect a set of 90 faces, with 9 subjects (each with 10 face, varying expressions). Classification accuracies on this data set are very encouraging, and make the proposed approach a promising really employable system for face recognition and authentication.

The rest of the paper is organized as follows: in the Sect. 2 the acquisition system is detailed, while in the recognition system is described in Sect. 3. The experimental evaluation is proposed in 4; finally, Sect. 5 contains conclusions and future perspectives.

2   The Acquisition System

Three-dimensional data are obtained from an active stereo system developed at
the VIPS (Vision, Image Processing, and Sound) laboratory[1] of the Department
of Computer Science (University of Verona). The system is composed by two
optical cameras and a overhead projector which illuminates the scene with a
salt-and-pepper random texture (Figure 1). Thus, all the surfaces are textured,

Fig. 1. Active Stereo system of acquisition

and every small surface patch is characterized by a very distinctive pattern
(Figure 2(a) and (b)). This trick facilitate area-based stereo matching, which
would otherwise produces no meaningful results for uniformly colored areas. In
summary, the acquisition pipeline is composed of the following stages:

Calibration. The position and orientation of both cameras, as well as intrinsic
parameters are computed with the calibration algorithm described in [15]
and implemented in a Matlab toolbox[2].

Rectification. Instead of relying on accurate mechanical alignment, a parallel-
camera acquisition geometry is "simulated" by transforming the images captured by the two cameras as if they were taken by two virtual parallel cameras. This process is called *epipolar rectification*, and is described in [16].

Stereo Matching. Corresponding points on the left and right images are recovered using the R-SMW area-based stereo matching algorithm [17]. However,
given that we project an artificial texture onto the scene, the choice of the
matching algorithm is less critical than in passive stereo.

The output of the system is a *disparity map* [10] related to the acquired subject
(Figure 2(c)). It is worth noting that the disparity map is very similar to a range

---

[1] See http://vips.sci.univr.it.
[2] The Camera Calibration Toolbox for Matlab is downloadable from
http://newbologna.vision.caltech.edu/bouguetj

map [18] and it covers the 3D information we are using for recognizing the faces. In particular light disparity pixels correspond to surface points that are closer to the sensor and vice versa.

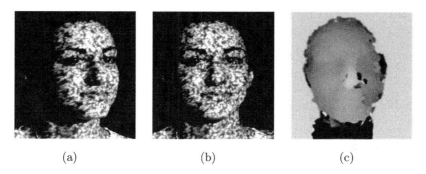

(a)   (b)   (c)

Fig. 2. Stereo images, left(a) and right (b), acquired while the overhead projector projects a random texture to the subject, and disparity map (c)

3   The Classification System

The classification system is based on two stages: firstly, range images are modelled using Multilevel B-Splines [11] and coefficients of approximation are extracted. Then, these coefficients are used for classification with Support Vector Machines [12].

3.1   Multilevel B-Splines

The *Multilevel B-Splines* [11] represent an approximation and interpolation technique for scattered data. More formally, let $\Omega = \{(x, y)|0 \leq x \leq m, 0 \leq y \leq n\}$ be a rectangular non-integer domain in the xy plane. Consider a set of scattered data points $P = \{(x_c, y_c, z_c)\}$ in 3D space, where (x_c, y_c) is a point in Ω. The *approximation function* f is defined as a regular B-Spline function, defined by a control lattice Φ overlaid to Ω, visualized in Fig. 3. Let Φ be a $(m+3) \times (n+3)$ lattice that spans the integer grid Ω.

The *approximation B-Spline function* is defined in terms of these control points by:

$$f(x, y) = \sum_{k=0}^{3} \sum_{l=0}^{3} B_k(s)B_l(t)\phi_{(i+k)(j+l)} \tag{1}$$

where $i = \lfloor x \rfloor - 1$, $j = \lfloor y \rfloor - 1$, $s = x - \lfloor x \rfloor$, $t = y - \lfloor y \rfloor$, ϕ_{ij} are control points, obtained as weighted sums with B-Spline coefficients B_k and B_l of 4×4 set of points, called proximity sets, belonging to Ω:

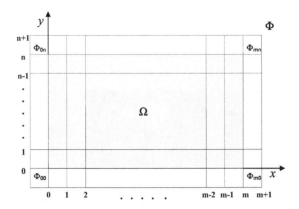

Fig. 3. Configuration of control lattice Φ in relation to domain Ω.

$$\phi_{ij} = \frac{\sum_c w_c^2 \phi_c}{\sum_c w_c^2} \qquad (2)$$

where $w_c = w_{kl} = B_k(s)B_l(t)$, $k = (i + 1) - \lfloor x_c \rfloor$, $l = (j + 1) - \lfloor y_c \rfloor$, $s = x_c - \lfloor x_c \rfloor$, $t = y_c - \lfloor y_c \rfloor$, (x_c, y_c, z_c) control points and $\phi_c = \frac{w_c z_c}{\sum_{a=0}^{3} \sum_{b=0}^{3} w_{ab}^2}$. By properly choosing the resolution of the control lattice Φ, it is possible to obtain a compromise between the precision and smoothness of the function; a good smoothness entails a cost in terms of low accuracy, and vice-versa.

Multilevel B-Splines approximation can overcome this problem. Consider a hierarchy of control lattices $\Phi_0, \Phi_1, \ldots, \Phi_h$, that spans the domain Ω. Assume that, having fixed the resolution of Φ_0, the spacing between control points in Φ_i is halved from one lattice to the next.

The process of approximation starts by applying the basic B-Spline approximation to P with the coarsest control lattice Φ_0, obtaining a smooth initial approximation f_0. f_0 leaves a deviation $\Delta^1 z_c = z_c - f_0(x_c, y_c)$ for each point (x_c, y_c, z_c) in P. Then, f_1 is calculated by the control lattice Φ_1, approximating the difference $P_1 = \{(x_c, y_c, \Delta_c^1)\}$. The sum $f_1 + f_2$ yields a smaller deviation $\Delta^2 z_c = z_c - f_0(x_c, y_c) - f_1(x_c, y_c)$ for each point (x_c, y_c, z_c) in P.

In general, for every level k in the hierarchy, using the control lattice Φ_k, a function f_k is derived to approximate data points $P_k = \{(x_c, y_c, \Delta^k z_c)\}$, where $\Delta^k z_c = z_c - \sum_{i=0}^{k-1} f_i(x_c, y_c)$, and $\Delta^0 z_c = z_c$. This process starts with the coarsest control lattice Φ_0 up to the highest lattice Φ_h. The final function f is calculated by the sum of functions f_k, $f = \sum_{k=0}^{h} f_k$.

In general, the higher the resolution of the coarsest control lattice Φ_0, the lower the smoothness of the final function. Given a set of points in a domain $width \times height$, m and n indicate that the lattice Φ, on which the approximating function has been built, has dimension $\left(\lfloor \frac{width}{m} \rfloor + 3 \right) \times \left(\lfloor \frac{height}{n} \rfloor + 3 \right)$. It follows that high values of m and n indicate low dimensions of Φ.

In the basic Multilevel B-Splines algorithm, the evaluation of f involves the computation of the function f_k for each level k, summing them over domain Ω. This introduces a significant overhead in computational time, if f has to be evaluated at a large number of points in Ω. To address this problem, Multilevel B-Splines refinement has been proposed in [11]. This technique allows to represent f by one B-Spline function rather than by the sum of several B-Spline functions.

Let $F(\Phi)$ be the B-spline function generated by control lattice Φ and let $|\Phi|$ denote the size of Φ. With B-spline refinement, we can derive the control lattice Φ'_0 from the coarsest lattice Φ_0 such that $F(\Phi'_0) = f_0$ and $|\Phi'_0| = |\Phi_1|$. Then, the sum of functions f_0 and f_1 can be represented by control lattice Ψ_1 which results from the addition of each corresponding pair of control points in Φ'_0 and Φ_1. That is, $F(\Psi_1) = g_1 = f_0 + f_1$, where $\Psi_1 = \Phi'_0 + \Phi_1$.

In general, let $g_k = \sum_{i=0}^{k} f_i$ be the partial sum of functions f_i up to level k in the hierarchy. Suppose that function g_{k-1} is represented by a control lattice Ψ_{k-1} such that $|\Psi_{k-1}| = |\Phi_{k-1}|$. In the same manner as we computed Ψ_1 above, n refine Ψ_{k-1} to obtain Ψ'_{k-1}, and add Ψ'_{k-1} to Φ_k to derive Ψ_k such that $F(\Psi_k) = g_k$ and $|\Psi_k| = |\Phi_k|$. That is, $\Psi_k = \Psi'_{k-1} + \Phi_k$. Therefore, from $g_0 = f_0$ and $\Psi_0 = \Phi_0$, we can compute a sequence of control lattices Ψ_k to progressively derive control lattice Ψ_h for the final approximation function $f = g_h$.

3.2   Support Vector Machines

Support Vector Machines [12] are binary classifiers, able to separate two classes through an optimal hyperplane. The optimal hyperplane is the one maximizing the "margin", defined as the distance between the closest examples of different classes. To obtain a non-linear decision surface, it is possible to use *kernel functions*, in order to project data in a high dimensional space, where a hyperplane can more easily separate them. The corresponding decision surface in the original space is not linear.

The rest of this section details the theoretical and practical aspects of Support Vector Machines: firstly, linear SVMs are introduced, for both linearly and not linearly separable data. Subsequently, we introduce non linear SVMs, able to produce non linear separation surfaces. A very useful and introductory tutorial on Support Vector Machines for Pattern Recognition can be found in [12].

In the case of linearly separable data, let $D = \{(\mathbf{x_i}, y_i)\}, i = 1 \ldots \ell, y_i \in \{-1, +1\}, \mathbf{x_i} \in \Re^d$ be the *training set* of the SVMs. D is linearly separable if exists $\mathbf{w} \in \Re^d$ and $b \in \Re$, such that:

$$y_i(\mathbf{x_i} \cdot \mathbf{w} + b) \geq 1 \text{ for } i = 1, \ldots, \ell \tag{3}$$

$H : \mathbf{w} \cdot \mathbf{x} + b = 0$ is called the "separating hyperplane". Let $d_+(d_-)$ be the minimum distance of the separating hyperplane from the closest positive (negative) point. Let us define the "margin" of the hyperplane as $d_+ + d_-$. Different separating hyperplanes exist. SVMs find the one that maximizes the margin. Let us define $H_1 : \mathbf{w} \cdot \mathbf{x} + b = +1$ and $H_2 : \mathbf{w} \cdot \mathbf{x} + b = -1$. The distance of a point of H_1 from $H : \mathbf{w} \cdot \mathbf{x} + b = 0$ is $\frac{|\mathbf{w} \cdot \mathbf{x} + b|}{\|\mathbf{w}\|} = \frac{1}{\|\mathbf{w}\|}$, and the distance between H_1 and

H_2 is $\frac{2}{\|\mathbf{w}\|}$. So, to maximize the margin, we must minimize $\|\mathbf{w}\| = \mathbf{w}^T\mathbf{w}$, with the constraints that no points lie between H_1 and H_2.

It can be proven [12] that the problem of training a SVM is reduced to the solution of the following Quadratic Programming (QP) problem:

$$\max\{-\frac{1}{2}\alpha^T B\alpha + \sum_{i=1}^{\ell}\alpha_i\} \tag{4}$$

$$\sum_{i=1}^{\ell} y_i\alpha_i = 0 \text{ and } \alpha_i \geq 0 \tag{5}$$

where α_i are Lagrange coefficients and B is a $\ell \times \ell$ matrix defined as:

$$B_{ij} = y_i y_j \mathbf{x_i} \cdot \mathbf{x_j} \tag{6}$$

The optimal hyperplane is determined with $\mathbf{w} = \sum_{i=1}^{\ell}\alpha_i y_i \mathbf{x_i}$, and the classification of a new point $\mathbf{x}$ is obtained by calculating $sgn(\mathbf{w}\cdot\mathbf{x}+b)$. It is important to observe that only those $\mathbf{x_i}$ whose corresponding Lagrange coefficients α_i are not null contribute to the sum that defines the separating hyperplane. For this reason, these points are called *support vectors* and, geometrically, lie along the two hyperplanes H_1 and H_2 (see the Fig. 4). When data points are not lin-

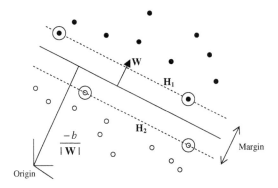

Fig. 4. Geometric interpretation of SVMs. A hyperplane separates black points from white points. The hyperplane is obtained as a linear combination of the circled points, called *support vectors*, and is defined by a direction vector $\mathbf{W}$ and a distance-from-origin scalar b.

early separable, slack variables are introduced, in order to allow points to exceed margin borders:

$$y_i(\mathbf{x_i}\cdot\mathbf{w}+b) \geq 1 - \xi_i \tag{7}$$

The idea is to permit such situations, by controlling them by the introduction of a cost parameter C. This parameter determines the sensibility of the SVM to classification errors: a high value of C strongly penalizes errors, also at the cost of a narrow margin, while a low value of C permits some classification errors. Intermediate values of C result in a compromise between the minimization of the number of errors and maximization of the margin. Finally, the training process results in the solution of the following QP problem:

$$\max \sum_i \alpha_i - \frac{1}{2} \sum_{i,j} \alpha_i \alpha_j y_i y_j \mathbf{x_i} \cdot \mathbf{x_j} \tag{8}$$

$$\sum_{i=1}^{\ell} y_i \alpha_i = 0 \text{ and } 0 \leq \alpha_i \leq C \tag{9}$$

The SVM approach could also be generalized to the case where the decision function is not a linear function of the data: in this case we have the so-called non-linear SVM. The idea under nonlinear SVMs is to project data points into a high, even huge, dimensional Hilbert space H, by using a function Ξ such that:

$$\Xi : \Re^d \to H$$
$$\mathbf{x} \to z(\mathbf{x}) = \mathbf{z}(\xi_1(\mathbf{x}), \xi_2(\mathbf{x}), \dots, \xi_n(\mathbf{x}))$$

and then separate projected data points through a hyperplane.

First of all, notice that the only way in which the data appear in the training problem is in the form of inner products $\mathbf{x_i} \cdot \mathbf{x_j}$. When projecting points $\mathbf{x}$ in $\Xi(\mathbf{x})$, the training process will still depend on the inner product of projected points $\Xi(\mathbf{x_i}) \cdot \Xi(\mathbf{x_j})$. Then, to solve the problem of nonlinear decision surfaces, it is sufficient to modify the training and classification algorithms, substituting the inner product between data points of the training set with a *kernel* function K, such that:

$$K(\mathbf{x_i}, \mathbf{x_j}) = \Xi(\mathbf{x_i}) \cdot \Xi(\mathbf{x_j}) \tag{10}$$

To be a *kernel*, a function must verify *Mercer conditions* [12]. Some examples of *kernel* are *polynomial functions* like $K(x, y) = ((x \cdot y) + 1)^d$, *exponential radial basis function* and *multi-layer perceptron*. In this way, data points are projected in a higher dimensional space, where a hyperplane could be sufficient to separate the problem properly. It is important to notice that, by the use of this "kernel trick", the non linear decision surface is obtained in roughly the same amount of time needed to build a linear SVM.

3.3   The Classification Strategy

For recognizing 3D faces we have employed the following strategy: firstly, the face surface is sampled, in order to obtain a set of points to approximate. Subsequently, the Multilevel B-Spline Algorithm with refinement (that is a variation to the basic algorithm described in [11]) is applied to this set of points, considering the control lattice coefficients of a certain level as features. Once extracted, the control lattice is linearized into a feature vector, using the standard raster scan.

Face recognition is a multi-class classification problem, but Support Vector Machines are binary classifiers. To extend SVMs to the multi-class case, we adopted the strategy of binary decision trees proposed by Verri *et al.* [13], called strategy of the tennis tournament, also adopted by Guo *et al.* in their paper [19].

Let us assume to have c classes. The training stage consists in building up all possible SVMs 1-vs-1[3], combining all the available classes. The number of possible (not ordered) pairs of classes is $\frac{c(c-1)}{2}$. In this way, $\frac{c(c-1)}{2}$ SVMs are trained. In the classification stage, a binary decision tree is built, starting from the leaves, in which each pair of brother nodes represent a SVM. Given a test image, recognition was performed following the rules of a tennis tournament. Each class is regarded as a player, and in each match the system classifies the test images according to the decision of the SVM of the pair of players involved in the match. The winner identities, proposed by each SVM, will be propagated to the upper level of the tree, playing again. The process continues until the root is reached. Finally, the root will be labelled with the identity of the classified subject. Because it is *a priori* impossible to know which SVM will define the various levels of the tree, the necessity of training all possible SVMs 1-vs-1 is now clear.

In Fig. 5, an example of this classification rule is proposed. In principle, different choices of the starting configuration, regarding SVMs inserted as leaves,

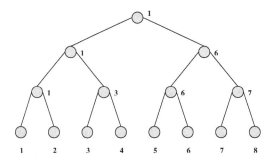

Fig. 5. An example of multi-class classification.The subject to be recognized belongs to class number 1. First, it is classified by the SVM relative to classes 1-2, 3-4, 5-6, 7-8. The winners of this first set of classifications will define the upper level of the tree, constituted by SVMs relative to pairs 1-3 and 6-7. Finally, the final SVM relative to classes 1 and 6 establishes the winner.

could lead to different results. Nevertheless, in practice, preliminary experiments showed that averaged accuracies do not depend from the starting configuration.

---

[3] We call this kind of SVMs 1-vs-1, in order to distinguish them from SVMs 1-vs-all, that were trained to classify between faces of one class and faces of all other classes.

If c does not equal to the power of 2, we can decompose c as: $c = 2^{n_1} + 2^{n_2} + \ldots + 2^{n_I}$, where $n_1 \geq n_2 \geq \ldots \geq n_I$. If c is an odd number, $n_I = 0$; otherwise, $n_I > 0$. Then, we can build I trees, the first with n_1 leaves, the second with n_2 and so on. Finally, starting from the I roots, we can build the final tree (or, if necessary, recursively decompose I again in powers of 2). Even if this decomposition is not unique, the number of comparisons in the classification stage is always $c - 1$.

4   Experimental Results

The system has been preliminary tested on a set of 9 subjects, each with 10 images, varying expression. Five images were used for the training, while the remaining were used for the testing. The parameters of the approach has been chosen based of a previous analysis on a 2D face recognition problem [14]: the coefficients level of the Multilevel B-splines approximation was set to 16. The SVM was used with the exponential Radial Basis Function kernel, using $\sigma = 10$. The C parameter, which drives the regularization [20], was set to 5. With 150×150 pixel images, the dimensionality of the control lattice, corresponding to the level 16, equals to $\left(\lfloor \frac{150}{16} \rfloor + 3 \right) \times \left(\lfloor \frac{150}{16} \rfloor + 3 \right) = 144$. Considering that images contain $150 \times 150 = 22.500$ pixels, level 16 permits a really noticeable dimensionality reduction, equal to about two orders of magnitude, precisely 99,36%.

Results are presented in Table 1, for different combination of the training and the testing set. We can note that results are very promising, in two cases

Training set	Recognition Error Rate
1st	0%
2nd	2.22%
3rd	2.22%
4th	2.22%
5th	2.22%
6th	0%

Table 1. Recognition Error Rates on 6 different combinations of training and testing sets.

the system reaches a perfect classification accuracy, and in the others it makes only one error. Clearly only nine subjects for the testing phase are not enough to have statistically significant results: nevertheless, a first impression about the performances of the proposed approach could be derived, giving a promising confidence for future developments. Anyway, a more deep testing, involving more subjects and more environmental changes, will be topic of future investigations.

5   Conclusions

In this paper a new complete low cost system for 3D face recognition has been presented. The 3D face is acquired using a stereo methodology, that does not require any expensive range sensors. The classification step is performed using Support Vector Machines and Multilevel B-Splines coefficients. Preliminary experimental evaluation has produced encouraging results, making the proposed system a promising low cost face recognition system.

References

1. Chellappa, R., Wilson, C., Sirohey, S.: Human and machine recognition of faces: a survey. Proceedings of IEEE **83** (1995) 705–740
2. Ming-Hsuan, Y., Kriegman, D., Ahuja, N.: Detecting faces in images: a survey. IEEE Trans. on Pattern Analysis and Machine Intelligence **24** (2002) 34–58
3. Ho-Chao, H., Ming, O., Wu, J.L.: Automatic feature point extraction on a human face in model-based image coding. Optical Engineering **32** (1993) 1571–1580
4. Lapresté, J., Cartoux, J., Richetin, M.: Face recognition from range data by structural analysis. In: Syntactic and Structural Pattern Recognition, NATO ASI Series (1988) 303–314
5. Gordon, G.: Face Recognition from depth and curvature. PhD thesis, Harvard University (1991)
6. Gordon, G.: Face recognition based on depth and curvature features. In: Proc. of Int. Conf. on Computer Vision and Pattern Recognition. (1992) 808–810
7. Achermann, B., Jiang, X., Bunke, H.: Face recognition using range images. In: Proc. of Int. Conf. on Virtual Systems and MultiMedia. (1997) 129–136
8. Achermann, B.: Face recognition using range images. PhD thesis, Institute of Computer Science and Applied Mathematics, University of Bern (1998)
9. Achermann, B., Bunke, H.: Classifying range images of human faces with hausdorff distance. In: Proc. of Int. Conf. on Pattern Recognition. Volume 2. (2000) 809–813
10. Dhond, U.R., Aggarwal, J.K.: Structure from stereo – a review. IEEE Trans. on System Man and Cybernetics **19** (1989) 1489–1510
11. Lee, S., Wolberg, G., Shin, S.Y.: Scattered data interpolation with multilevel b-splines. IEEE Trans. on Visualization and Computer Graphics **3** (1997) 228–244
12. Burges, C.: A tutorial on support vector machine for pattern recognition. Data Mining and Knowledge Discovery **2** (1998) 121–167
13. Pontil, M., Verri, A.: Support vector machines for 3-d object recognition. IEEE Trans. on Pattern Analysis and Machine Intelligence **20** (1998) 637–646
14. Bicego, M., Iacono, G., Murino, V.: Face recognition with multilevel b-splines and support vector machines. In: Proc. of ACM SIGMM Multimedia Biometrics Methods and Applications Workshop. (2003)
15. Zhang, Z.: Flexible camera calibration by viewing a plane from unknown orientations. In: Proc. of Int. Conf. on Computer Vision, Corfu, Greece (1999)
16. Fusiello, A., Trucco, E., Verri, A.: A compact algorithm for rectification of stereo pairs. Machine Vision and Applications **12** (2000) 16–22
17. Fusiello, A., Castellani, U., Murino, V.: Relaxing symmetric multiple windows stereo using markov random fields. In M.Figureido, Zerubia, J., Jain, A., eds.: Energy Minimization Methods in Computer Vision and Pattern Recognition. Number 2124 in Lecture Notes in Computer Science, Springer (2001) 91–104

18. Trucco, E., Verri, A.: Introductory Techniques for 3-D Computer Vision. Prentice-Hall (1998)
19. Guo, G., Li, S.Z., , Kapluk, C.: Face recognition by support vector machines. Image and Vision Computing **19** (2001) 631–638
20. Vapnik, V.: The Nature of Statistical Learning Theory. Springer-Verlag (1995)

Selection of Location, Frequency, and Orientation Parameters of 2D Gabor Wavelets for Face Recognition

Berk Gökberk, M. Okan Irfanoglu, Lale Akarun, and Ethem Alpaydın

Boğaziçi University, Department of Computer Engineering,
TR-34342, Istanbul, Turkey
{gokberk, irfanoglu, akarun, alpaydin}@boun.edu.tr

Abstract. In this paper, a two–level supervised feature selection algorithm for local feature–based face recognition is presented. In the first part, a genetic algorithm is used to determine the useful locations of the face region for recognition. 2D Gabor wavelet–based feature extractors are used for local image descriptors at these locations. In the second part, the most useful frequencies and orientations of Gabor kernels are determined using a floating feature selection algorithm. Our major aim in this study is to examine the relevance of the two common assumptions in the local feature based face recognition literature: first, that the contribution of a specific feature to the recognition performance is independent of others, and secondly, that feature extractors should be placed over the visually salient points. In this paper, we show that one can obtain better recognition accuracy by relaxing these two assumptions.

1 Introduction

In all of the computational face processing tasks such as face recognition, detection, and tracking, it is now widely accepted that the representation of a human face plays a very important role. In much of the recent works, researchers try to find an efficient representation method for a given task. In the face recognition literature, several approaches emerged during the last few years. These approaches can be broadly classified into two groups: local feature–based approaches including template–based methods, and global statistical approaches[1].

Feature–based approaches try to code face images using several different methodologies. In the most simplistic way, one can represent a face image using geometrical relations among various face regions. As this method, most feature–based approaches try to localize various facial feature points, such as the coordinates of eyes, mouth, nose, and eyebrows. Once these points are found or tracked, you can represent the face image by features extracted from these points.

2D Gabor wavelet–based methods are frequently used in feature–based face representation approaches as local feature extractors. Gabor kernels are similar to the receptive fields of simple cells in the primary visual cortex. In addition, multi–resolution and multi-orientation capabilities of Gabor kernels make them

M. Tistarelli, J. Bigun, and E. Grosso (Eds.): Biometrics School 2003, LNCS 3161, pp. 138–146, 2005.

attractive for face representation. Since the full convolution of face images with different Gabor kernels is very costly, sparse sampling is generally used where local feature vectors are formed at each positions of Gabor kernels.

Typically, the features extracted by 2D Gabor wavelets have a very large dimensionality. It is, therefore, essential to analyze the contribution of each feature component to performance of the task at hand. In the most general case, one should examine three parameters of a Gabor kernel: location, frequency and orientation [2, 3].

There were several studies that tried to emphasize the importance of Gabor kernel parameters for face recognition. In [4], the discriminative power of the nodes of a graph that is placed over face features is examined. The aim is to learn the weights of nodes for face discrimination. The problem is formulated as an optimization problem and simplex algorithm is used. According to their results, the eyes are more important for discrimination of half profiles and frontal faces compared to the mouth and chin. A similar approach was employed in [5] where the aim of the learning algorithm is to find out a suitable subgraph which only contains the nodes important for head finding and pose identification.

In a recent statistical analysis of 2D Gabor wavelet–based feature detectors [6], univariate analysis of variance of 2D Gabor kernel activations has been used to weight the contribution of each parameter (kernel location, frequency, and orientation) in the representation according to its power of predicting similarity of faces. The results show that the hairline area with the forehead and eye regions provide useful information while the mouth, nose, cheek and lower part of the outline region are the least useful part of a face for face recognition. In a similar work, results confirm that the eyes and mouth are more stable for recognition, whereas hair and nose region have large variations [7].

In almost all of the previous studies, either the importance of the locations of Gabor kernels or the importance of the used frequencies and orientations are examined. Only in [6], all the three parameters are examined, but they assume the independence of each feature dimension. This independence assumption is actually not valid, so one needs a more complex methodology to infer the usefulness of each local feature element. In this paper, we have formalized our approach as a subset selection problem, and removed the independence assumption. In addition, we also wanted to show the validity of the commonly used sampling technique of placing the Gabor kernels at salient facial feature positions such as the corners of eyes, mouth and the tip of the nose, etc. In the rest of the paper, we explain our local image descriptors in section 2, and feature selection methodology in section 3. In section 4, we give experimental results for FERET face database.

2   Image Representation Using 2D Gabor Wavelets

Local features are represented using the convolution results of the face image with 2D Gabor wavelets at the convolution points. At each image point, we have convolved the image with Gabor kernels having five different frequencies and eight different orientations. The Gabor kernel resolution is selected as 15×15 pixels in order to reduce the overlapping of kernels. The magnitudes of complex outputs of Gabor convolutions are used as feature descriptors, giving a feature vector of size 40 at each image point.

There are several methods to represent whole image using local jets. At one extreme, images can be represented by the full convolution with Gabor kernels at each pixel. Another approach would be to place a face graph where the nodes of the graph lie on facial features. This approach requires a fine localization of facial feature points. In between these two approaches, one can use a rectangular sampling grid that is placed over the face region.

3   Feature Selection Methodology

In feature selection, the goal is to find a subset maximizing a selected criterion. This criterion can be inter–class distance measure or the classification rate of a classifier. The optimal solution could be found by using exhaustive search. However, for higher dimensional problems, this solution is unusable. Branch and bound type of algorithms can also give optimal solutions [8], but their application is only limited to monotonic criterion functions, which does not hold in our case. Alternative to optimal algorithms, several fast sub–optimal algorithms can be used. Among them, the most frequently used ones are: sequential forward selection (SFS), sequential backward selection (SBS), plus–L–minus–R, and floating search methods (SFFS, SFBS) [9]. Genetic algorithms (GA) and tabu search are also proposed as solutions for a subset selection problem [9].

In order to apply feature selection algorithms to the task of finding optimal Gabor kernel locations, and finding useful frequency/orientation parameters, we have decomposed the problem into two parts by separating location finding problem and frequency/orientation selection problem. In the first part, location selection module tries to find optimal face regions in a supervised manner by using all of the 40 different Gabor kernels having full frequency and orientation range. Then, in the second part, frequency and orientation selection module tries to come up with an efficient subset of all of the different Gabor kernels at the nd locations.

3.1   Kernel Location Selection

In order to find the most discriminative image locations of faces for recognition, we have designed several feature selection scenarios. These scenarios are, namely: best individual features (BIF), forward selection(SFS), floating forward search (SFFS), and genetic algorithm. In the first three approaches, we represented the face images using both rectangular grids (lattice) and manually positioned face graphs. Lattice–based sampling is done via placing a 7×7 grid centered on the face region. As a face graph, we have identified 30 facial feature points, as seen in Figure 2.a , and used them as the nodes of our graph. In the GA approach, we have used full convolutions of Gabor wavelets at each pixel in the image.

3.2 Kernel Frequency and Orientation Selection

After finding useful kernel locations, similar feature selection methodology as in the previous part should be carried out in order to eliminate irrelevant feature dimensions. For this purpose, we have applied another layer of SFFS–type feature selection mechanism to the outputs of the location selection module. Frequency and orientation selection module also works in a supervised manner, and it produces a subset of a useful frequencies and orientations at each kernel location. Since, we use all the information produced by location selection module together, without dividing them according to the kernel locations, this methodology also produces an almost optimal subset by taking into account the dependence of each feature dimension.

4 Experiments and Results

In our experiments, we have used a subset of the FERET face database [10]. The used part of the database contains normalized frontal images of 146 subjects. Each subject has 4 gray scale images of resolution 150×130. In all of the experiments, we have put 2 images of a subject into training set, and the rest of the images into test set. Faces in the dataset contain facial expression and illumination variations. In the recognition part, we have used 1–nearest neighbor classifier.

4.1 Kernel Location Selection

BIF, SFS, and SFFS Based Selection In a recognition problem, each individual local feature has a certain degree of recognition power. Therefore, it is useful to learn the importance of each local feature in order to obtain a better discriminator. The best heuristic to measure the importance of each local feature is to look at its individual recognition performance. In the BIF approach, one can simply combine the most important N features into a final feature vector. This simple idea can perform well only if each local descriptor contributes independently to the discrimination performance, irrespective of the existence of other local features. However, in many cases, it would be proper to design a feature selector which additionally takes into account the relative information gain when used with an existing feature set. Thus, we have used SFS algorithm in order to consider this relative gain. More formally, we add the most informative local feature at each step to an existing previously selected subset S.

SFFS algorithm takes this idea one step further by backtracking to remove the least useful features from an existing feature subset to overcome the nesting effect. Specifically, SFFS adds the most useful feature and then searches for a feature in the existing subset S to discard if the removal of that feature improves the discriminative power.

In our experiments, we have placed a rectangular lattice of size 7×7 over the face region, and look for a useful subset of grid points for efficient face representation for recognition task. In the second column of Table 1, the recognition performances of each method are presented. The recognition accuracies of BIF, SFS, and SFFS are 84.54, 90.38, and 91.07 percent respectively. The recognition performance of using all of the grid points is 86.94 percent. In Figures 1.a, 1.b and 1.c, the most important 15 local feature positions are shown for BIF, SFS, and SFFS algorithms. In Figure 1.a, circle sizes are proportional to each points recognition performance. The best performance is obtained using the SFFS approach, where the selected subset performs even better than using all of the grid points, and as expected, BIF approach performed worst among all of these methods since it considers each feature independently.

In all of the three approaches, most of the selected grid points are at the upper part of the face region. This result is largely due to the expression variations present in the dataset especially, in the mouth region. In SFFS, the combination of features extracted from eyebrows, the lower–center part of the forehead, the nose region, and the lower part of the mouth seems important.

Table 1. Comparative analysis of BIF, SFS, and SFFS for lattice– and face graph–based sampling methods. The numbers in parentheses show the number of feature points for each representation

	Lattice (49 pts)	Face Graph (30 pts)
All pts	86.94	83.85
BIF (15 pts)	84.54	82.13
SFS (15 pts)	90.38	87.97
SFFS (15 pts)	91.07	87.97

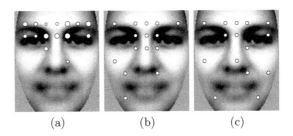

(a)   (b)   (c)

Fig. 1. The locations of important facial feature combinations for a) BIF, b) SFS, and c) SFFS approaches. The grid size in all figures is 7×7. The recognition performances are 84.54, 90.38, and 91.07 percent, respectively.

Similarly, we have performed the same feature selection analysis to the manually positioned face graph, in order to see the importance of the generally used fiducial points. In the third column of Table 1, the recognition accuracies of BIF,

SFS, and SFFS is shown. Using all of the 30 points in the face graph gives 83.85 percent classification performance, whereas an SFS-, or SFFS-based subset selection can improve the performance to 87.97 percent. In Figures 2.b, 2.c, and 2.c, the locations of 15 useful fiducial points are shown. The points selected for SFS and SFFS methods are the same, and they are generally at the upper face region. Eyebrows, the corners of eyes, forehead, cheeks, and the outline of nose seem to carry the most discriminative information.

When lattice and face graph based sampling is considered, lattice–based approach performs better. Our results show that although fiducial points are important, feature selection from a set of fiducial points greatly improves performance. Furthermore, our experiments with the lattice approach show that superior results can be achieved at the periphery of fiducial points.

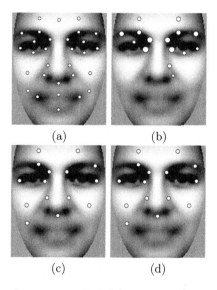

Fig. 2. The locations of important facial feature combinations for manually positioned face graph. a) the locations of 30 fiducial points used, b) subset of 15 points for BIF c) subset of 15 points for SFS, d) subset of 15 points for SFFS. The recognition performances are 82.13, 87.97, and 87.97 percent, respectively.

Genetic Algorithm–Based Selection One of the key motivations of our research was to try to understand whether it is better to choose the locations of facial features for local image descriptors. Therefore, we aimed to search for useful combination of face locations from data, without using any a priori information, such as fiducial point coordinates. In contrast to the sparse sampling methods (lattice, face graph), we have a much larger search space. The complexity of the search space is determined by the exhaustive search of a combination of N feature points selected from all of the pixels in the face region. However, in higher dimensions, such as in our problem, exhaustive search is unusable. So, we have used a genetic algorithm which is sub–optimal but faster. It was shown that genetic algorithms can reach near–optimal solutions quickly in feature selection [9].

In our setting, genetic chromosomes contain the coordinates of the selected number of face locations. We decided to use 15 points for face representation. As fitness function, we have used the recognition performance of local image descriptors of each gene in the chromosomes. The crossover and mutation parameters are 0.5 and 0.1, respectively. In both operators, we require that the coordinates of face points in a single chromosome do not overlap too much in order to extract independent local information as much as possible. This minimum overlap distance between facial point is selected to be 9 pixels. Mutation of a gene is handled by adding a random number within a specified range. This range is dependent on the image resolution. As the populations evolve, we iteratively narrow this range for better convergence. The selection of new population is based on the probability distribution of fitness values of each chromosome. For quick convergence, elitism is employed, where the elitism ratio is 0.05. As an initial population size, 200 is used.

In Figure 3, the 15 feature points found by the GA is shown. The recognition performance of this feature subset is 96.50 percent which is even better than the best sequential feature selection algorithm, namely SFFS. Again, all of the feature points are gathered over the upper face region. Similar to results of the SFFS algorithm, the outer corners of eyebrows, forehead region, and the outline of nose provide the most useful information.

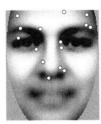

Fig. 3. The locations of important facial feature combinations for genetic algorithm.

4.2   Kernel Frequency and Orientation Selection

In the second part of our two–level feature selection approach, we determine the most useful orientations and frequencies of the selected kernel locations using SFFS–based methodology. The output of the kernel location module is a feature vector of size 15×40, where each kernel contributes only one jet having a dimension of 15. In frequency and orientation selection part, we further study an efficient subset of the output of the kernel location module. Therefore, in applying SFFS, we start with an empty set of selected features, and gradually add additional features. Note that, each added dimension corresponds to a specific frequency and orientation pair of the outputs of a previously selected Gabor kernel at some specific location. Again, the feature selection criteria in SFFS is the supervised classification accuracy of the selected subset.

Using this policy, we can extract a better feature subset of the original set, because of the large dimensionality of the original set. In order to find the near optimal subset, we have forced the SFFS algorithm to find a subset of dimension 600. Then, we select the minimal subset having a peak performance. In this way, we improved the performance of the face recognition system on the test set from 96.50 percent to 99.32 percent, by using a subset of dimensionality 230 out of 600.

5   Conclusion and Future Work

In this work, a methodology to represent human faces in a local feature–based approach is presented. Previous research on feature selection for face recognition mainly focuses on the individual, independent contribution of each face point to the recognition performance. We have shown that, it is better to formulate the problem as a feature subset selection, where the addition or subtraction of a feature point is evaluated with respect to an existing feature subset.

Another common assumption in previous approaches was to extract local features from fiducial points. To test the validity of this assumption, we have used different sampling methods coupled with different feature selection algorithms. Our results show that although fiducial points are important, feature selection from a set of fiducial points greatly improves performance, and superior recognition accuracy can be achieved at the periphery of fiducial points. As a second phase, we have introduced a selection of frequency and orientation parameters using a sequential floating subset search. By extracting useful frequencies and orientations at specific face locations, we have eliminated the irrelevant parts of the original feature vector, and also improved the recognition performance significantly.

In our experiments, sequential forward selection algorithm and genetic algorithm gave the best performances, while the latter is superior to the SFFS. In order to compare their performance with methods that selects features based solely on their individual importance, we have implemented Best Individual Feature (BIF) algorithm. As expected, both SFFS and GA outperformed BIF–based feature selection. In general, eyebrows and face points at the outline of nose seem to provide the most discriminatory information for face recognition. As future work, we will extend this methodology for pose invariant face recognition.

References

[1] Chellappa, R., Wilson, C.L., Sirohey, S.: Human and machine recognition of faces: A survey. Proceedings of IEEE **83** (1995) 705–740

[2] Gokberk, B., Akarun, L., Alpaydin, E.: Feature selection for pose invariant face recognition. In: Proceedings of the 16th Iinternational Conference on Pattern Recognition. (2002)

[3] Gokberk, B., Irfanoglu, M.O., Akarun, L., Alpaydin, E.: Optimal gabor kernel location selection for face recognition. In: Proceedings of the IEEE International Conference on Image Processing. (2003)

[4] Kruger, N.: An algorithm for the learning of weights in discrimination functions using a priori constraint. IEEE Transactions on Pattern Analysis and Machine Intelligence **19** (1997) 764–768

[5] Kruger, N., Potzsch, M., Malsburg, C.: Determination of face position and pose with a learned representation based on labelled graphs. Image and Vision Computing **15** (1997) 665–673

[6] Kalocsai, P., Malsburg, C., Horn, J.: Face recognition by statistical analysis of feature detectors. Image and Vision Computing **18** (2000) 273–278

[7] Grudin, M.: On internal representations in face recognition. Pattern Recognition **33** (2000) 1161–1177

[8] Jain, A., Duin, R.P.W., Mao, J.: Statistical pattern recognition: a review. IEEE Transactions on Pattern Analysis and Machine Intelligence **22** (2000) 4–37

[9] Kudo, M., Sklansky, J.: Comparison of algorithms that select features for pattern classifiers. Pattern Recognition **33** (2000) 25–41

[10] Phillips, P.J., Wechsler, H., Huang, J., Rauss, P.: The feret database and evaluation procedure for face recognition algorithms. Image and Vision Computing **16** (1998) 295–306

A Face Recognition System Based on Local Feature Characterization

Paola Campadelli and Raffaella Lanzarotti

DSI - Università degli Studi di Milano
Via Comelico, 39/41 20135 Milano, Italy
{campadelli,lanzarotti}@dsi.unimi.it

Abstract. A completely automatic face recognition system is presented. The method works on color and gray level images: after having localized the face and the facial features, it determines 16 facial fiducial points, and characterizes them applying a bank of filters which extract the peculiar texture around them (*jets*). Recognition is realized measuring the similarity between the different *jets*. The system is inspired by the elastic bunch graph method, but the fiducial point localization does not require any manual setting.

1 Introduction

Human face recognition has been largely investigated for the last two decades; the most famous approaches adopt eigenfaces and neural networks.

In this paper we present an approach based on another technique: the elastic bunch graphs [3], but with a new and completely automatic method to localize sixteen facial fiducial points (the eyebrow and chin vertices, the nose tip, and the eye and lip corners and upper and lower middle points).

We build three galleries, each one containing an image per person: the frontal, right and left rotated face galleries. Given an image, the system extracts the fiducial points, characterizes them, determines the head pose, and compares the face with the proper gallery images. We observe that, while the face analysis is done on the gray levels only, the fiducial point extractor works on both color and gray level images, even if the one based on color is slightly more precise.

We present encouraging results obtained on databases of up to 200 subjects; 150 of them have been extracted from the FERET database, and 50 from our color image database. The considered sub-set of the FERET database consists in 8 gray level images per person organized according to the angle between the subjects and the camera ($0°$, $\pm15°$, $\pm25°$, $\pm40°$), and where two sets of frontal view images, respectively with neutral and smiling expression, are included. Our database consists in 6 images per person: two frontal, two right rotated and two left rotated, with a miscellaneous of rotation angles and approximately neutral expressions.

M. Tistarelli, J. Bigun, and E. Grosso (Eds.): Biometrics School 2003, LNCS 3161, pp. 147–152, 2005.

2   Face and Facial Features Localization

The first step consists in localizing the face in the image. In [1] we have presented a method which localizes faces in generic color images searching at first all the skin regions, and then validating the ones which contain at least one eye. Regarding gray level images, we have proposed a method [2] that works on images of face foregrounds with a homogeneous and light-colored background. Subsequently, the facial features (eyes, nose, mouth, and chin) are localized [2].

We have tested the methods on 500 color images, and 2000 gray level ones, obtaining correct results in the 95% of the cases.

3   Identification of Fiducial Points

In this section we describe the steps followed for the determination of the fiducial points. The eyes and mouth are described by two parametric models derived from the deformable templates proposed in [4] with significant variations.

Eyes. In the eye sub-image the iris is first identified with the Hough transform for circumferences and the reflex, often present in it, is eliminated. Without these preliminary steps the deformable template finds very often wrong contours. The template [Fig.1.1], described by 6 parameters $\{x_w, y_w, a, b, c, \theta\}$, is made of two parabolas representing the eye arcs and intersecting at the eye corners.

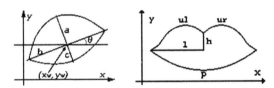

Fig. 1. Eye and Mouth Deformable templates.

As Yuille did, we define an energy function E_t to be minimized. E_t is the sum of three terms which are functions of the template parameters and of the image characteristics (prior information on the eye shape, edges, and 'white' of the eye). For color images, the characteristics are evaluated on the u plane of the CIE-Luv space. More precisely: $E_t = E_{prior} + E_e + E_i$, where:

1. $E_{prior} = \frac{k_1}{2} \left((x_w - x_i)^2 + (y_w - y_i)^2 \right) + \frac{k_2}{2} \cdot (b - 2r)^2 + \frac{k_3}{2} \left((b - 2a)^2 + (a - 2c)^2 \right)$

   (x_i, y_i) is the iris center and r the iris ray obtained by the Hough transform.

2. $E_e = -\frac{c_1}{|\partial R_w|} \cdot \int_{\partial R_w} \phi_e(\boldsymbol{x}) ds$

   ∂R_w represents the upper and lower parabolas, and ϕ_e is the edge image obtained applying the Sobel edge detector.

3. $E_i = -c_2 \int_{R_w} \phi_i(\boldsymbol{x}) ds$

where R_w is the region enclosed between the two parabolas, and ϕ_i is the binary image obtained applying an adaptive thresholding able to balance the number of white pixels on both sides of the iris. $\phi_i(p)$ is set to 255 if p is white, to -100 if p is black.

After this, we follow the Yuille's work obtaining a good eye description, and we extract from it the two eye corners and the upper and lower middle points.

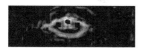

Fig. 2. Eye image processing: ϕ_e obtained from the u plane; ϕ_i obtained binarizing the u plane; Final result.

Mouth. In the mouth sub-image we calculate the mouth corners, and the entire border adopting a parametric model.

The mouth corners correspond to the extreme of the mouth cut, obtained combining the image vertical derivative, and the image low values [2].

The mouth model [Fig.1.2] is parameterized by $\{l, h, a_p, a_{ul}, b_{ul}, a_{ur}, b_{ur}\}$, and is made of one parabola, p, for the lower lip, and two cubics, ul and ur, for the upper lip. Two energy functions to be minimized are defined; both of them are functions of the template parameters but the first, E_i, depends on the image colors/gray levels, while the second, E_e, depends on the edge image (I_{Edges}). The model is modified in two epochs considering respectively the E_i and the E_e functions. More precisely:

1. $E_i = c_2 \int_R \phi_i(\boldsymbol{x}) dA$

   where R is the region enclosed among the 3 curves and ϕ_i is the binary image obtained clustering in 2 clusters the MouthMap (for gray level images, the MouthMap is the negative of the mouth sub-images itself, while for color images it is: $MouthMap = (255 - (C_r - C_b)) \cdot C_r^2$), and setting a pixel to 255 if it is white, to -80 if it is black.

2. $E_e = c_1(-\frac{100}{|ul|} \int_{ul} \phi_e(\boldsymbol{x}) ds - \frac{100}{|ur|} \int_{ur} \phi_e(\boldsymbol{x}) ds - \frac{10}{|p|} \int_p \phi_e(\boldsymbol{x}) ds), \quad \phi_e = I_{Edges}.$

Eyebrow and Chin. The eyebrow and chin description consists in the best parabola which approximates their vertical derivative [Fig. 3].

Nose. The nose is characterized by very simple and generic properties: the nose has a 'base' which gray levels contrast significantly with the neighbor regions; moreover, the nose profile can be characterized as the set of points with the highest symmetry and high luminance values; finally we can say that the nose tip lies on the nose profile, above the nose base line, and is bright [Fig. 3].

Fig. 3. Examples of facial feature and fiducial point description.

3.1   Experimental Results

The method has shown very good performances (error of 1 or 2 pixels) under some commonly accepted assumptions: the head image dimensions are not lower than (100×100) pixels; the head rotation is at most of $45°$; the mouth are closed and the eyes opened; the illumination is not too low, and does not create particular shadows on the faces.

We observe that errors of one or two pixels do not constitute critical problems for the subsequent steps, since both the face characterization and recognition are not based on the fiducial points punctual values, but on a local analysis of the regions around them, making the system more robust.

4   Face Dimension Normalization and Pose Determination

The previous steps have dealt with faces of any scale and different orientation; however the face characterization and recognition are very sensitive to these kind of variations. We thus proceed rescaling the images to a common size and determining the head rotation. To these purposes, we consider the triangle whose vertices are the nose tip (N_t) and the eye external corners (C_1, C_2). We first normalize the image so that the triangle area is of 2000 pixels; subsequently we compare the length of the two segments which connect N_t to C_1 and C_2 respectively. In case of frontal image, the two segments are approximately of the same length, while, when the head is rotated, the two lengths vary greatly and according to the rotation side. We thus recognize three different poses: frontal, right and left rotated.

5   Face Characterization

In order to characterize the fiducial points, we have experimented two techniques: the Gabor wavelet transform and the steerable Gaussian first derivative basis filters. The first technique has shown greater robustness with respect to rotation and little error in the fiducial point localization. We thus describe it only.

To characterize a fiducial point, we convolve the portion of gray image around it with a bank of *Gabor kernels*; following the idea of Wiskott [3], 5 different frequencies and 8 orientations are exployed. The obtained 40 coefficients are complex numbers. A *jet J* is obtained considering the magnitude parts only.

Applying the Gabor wavelet transform to all the facial fiducial points, we obtain the face characterization, consisting in a *jets vector* of $40 \times N$ real   ients where N is the number of visible fiducial points.

To recognize a face image I we compute a similarity measure between its *jets vector* and the ones of all the images G_i in the corresponding gallery, and we associate I to the G_i which maximizes the measure of similarity. Being J_n^i the *n-th* jet of the *jets vector* i, we define the similarity between two *jets vector* as:

$$S_v(V^1, V^2) = \frac{1}{N} \sum_{n=0}^{N-1} \frac{J_n^1 \cdot J_n^2}{\|J_n^1\| \|J_n^2\|}$$

6 Experimental Results

We have experimented the whole face recognition system on databases of 50, 100, 150, and 200 subjects. For each of them, three images are catalogued in the galleries according to the pose. Regarding the FERET database, the frontal and neutral expression image set, and the $\pm 40°$ image sets are used as gallery images, while the other are used to test the system. In the following, we report the most significant results.

At first, in order to highlight the system behavior according to the different rotation angles, we report the experiments carried out referring to the FERET images only. In particular, we give all the details for the most challenging experiment, and summary results for the other cases.

Analyzing the results exhibited in table 1, we notice that the system is more robust to little rotation disparity (e.g. second line) than to expression variations (first line). However, incrementing the rotation angle disparity, the performances decrease (e.g. sixth line); it thus arises the importance of having an automatic face pose estimator which allows to compare each test image to the gallery with the less angle disparity. The bold lines in the table reflect this choice.

In table 2 we report the recognition performance obtained using subsets of fiducial points. We remark that most of the discriminating face characteristics are in the upper part of the faces, above all if the face expression varies significantly (see first line of the table).

Finally we report the results obtained, referring to a gallery of 200 subjects (150 from the FERET database and 50 from our color image database), and using all the fiducial points to test the system. In the 92.5% of the cases the best match corresponded to the right person, while in 95.6% of the cases the correct person's face was in the top five candidate matches.

Gallery	Test	Best rank	In top 5
$0°$	$0°$	70	82
$0°$	$+15°$	94	96
$0°$	$-15°$	95	97
$0°$	$+25°$	90	96
$0°$	$-25°$	93	96
$+40°$	$+15°$	90	96
$+40°$	$+25°$	96	98
$-40°$	$-15°$	78	93
$-40°$	$-25°$	95	96

Table 1. Recognition results obtained referring to the 150-subject galleries, and exploiting all the 16 fiducial points.

Gallery	Test	Best rank		In top 5	
		EEH	MCH	EEH	MCH
$0°$	$0°$	26	68	46	79
$0°$	$+15°$	93	93	95	96
$0°$	$-15°$	89	92	95	95
$+40°$	$+25°$	81	91	91	95
$-40°$	$-25°$	72	93	82	95

Table 2. Recognition results obtained referring to the 150-subject galleries, in case of partial occlusions: **EEH**: eyes and eyebrows hidden; **MCH**: mouth and chin hidden.

7   Conclusions

We have presented a system that, given a face image, extracts the facial fiducial points, determines the head pose, normalizes the image, characterizes it with its *jets vector*, and compares it with the ones in the corresponding gallery. The image is recognized to be the most similar one in the gallery.

The facial feature detection and description methods have been tested on 2500 face foregrounds images detecting the fiducial points with high accuracy (errors of 1 or 2 pixels are negligible) in 93% of the images.

The whole face recognition system has been tested on a database of 1500 images of 200 subjects. We can affirm that our fiducial point extractor allows to obtain the same recognition performances as the elastic bunch graph used in [3], while being completely automatic.

References

1. P. Campadelli, F. Cusmai, and R. Lanzarotti. A color based method for face detection. *Submitted*, 2003.
2. P. Campadelli and R. Lanzarotti. Localization of facial features and fiducial points. *Processings of the International Conference Visualisation, Imaging and image Processing (VIIP2002), Malaga (Spagna)*, pages 491–495, 2002.
3. L. Wiskott, J. Fellous, N. Kruger, and C. von der Malsburg. Face recognition by elastic bunch graph matching. In L.C. Jain et al., editor, *Intelligent biometric techniques in fingerprints and face recognition*, pages 355–396. CRC Press, 1999.
4. A.L. Yuille, P.W. Hallinan, and D.S. Cohen. Feature extraction from faces using deformable templates. *International journal of computer vision*, 8(2):99–111, 1992.

Influence of Location over Several Classifiers in 2D and 3D Face Verification

Susana Mata[1], Cristina Conde[1], Araceli Sánchez[2], and Enrique Cabello[1]

[1] Universidad Rey Juan Carlos (ESCET)
C/Tulipán s/n
28933 Móstoles, Spain
[2] Universidad de Salamanca (Facultad de Ciencias)
Dpto. de Informática y Automática
Plaza de la Merced s/n
37008 Salamanca, Spain

Abstract. In this paper two methods for human face recognition and the influence of location mistakes are shown. First one, Principal Components Analysis (PCA), has been one of the most applied methods to perform face verification in 2D. In our experiments three classifiers have been considered to test influence of location errors in face verification using PCA. An initial set of "correct located faces" has been used for PCA matrix computation and to train all classifiers. An initial test set was built considering a "correct located faces" set (based on different images than training ones) and then a new test set was obtained by applying a small displacement in both axis (20 pixels) to the initial set. Second method is based on geometrical characteristics constructed with facial and cranial points that come from a 3D representation. Data are acquired by a calibrated stereo system. Classifiers considered for both methods are k-nearest neighbours (KNN), artificial neural networks: radial basis function (RBF) and Support Vector Machine (SVM). Given our data set, results show that SVM is capable to classify correctly in the presence of small location errors. RBF has an acceptable correct rate but the number of false positives is always higher than in the SVM case.

1 Introduction

In recent years three main approaches to face verification problem using only 2D information has appeared.

Principal Components Analysis (PCA) and related methods such as Fisherfaces [1] [2] Methods based on PCA consider only global information for the face. Using PCA, a dimensional reduction is performed in order to obtain a compact representation of the face.

Elastic Bunch Graph Matching (EBGM) [3] uses wavelet transformation to obtain local description of the face and a graph to obtain the global face description

Local Feature Analysis (LFA) [6], similar to PCA, considers different kernel functions to obtain local features (eyes, mouth and nose). In this case, selection of facial features and kernels is an open issue.

M. Tistarelli, J. Bigun, and E. Grosso (Eds.): Biometrics School 2003, LNCS 3161, pp. 153-158, 2005.

Research is also developed considering 3D information [5][6][7]. Laser scanners to obtain 3D data are very expensive, so a stereo pair was used to acquire the 3D data.

In our experiment, two methods of representing a face are considered: PCA in 2D representation and geometrical characteristics in 3D representation.

Principal Components Analysis offers a compact representation of the face, well suited for its transmission. in a distributed environment. On the other hand, PCA is quite sensitive to small displacements in face location. To observe the sensitivity of classifiers to these location errors, small displacements were introduced.

The 3D description is obtained by the calibration of a stereo pair of cameras for head navigation. The algorithm has been tested in the 3D reconstruction of real faces.

Experiments presented in this paper compare results obtained with three classifiers. K-Nearest Neighbours (KNN), artificial neural networks: Radial Basis Functions (RBF) and Support Vector Machine (SVM) [8].

2 Experimental Set Up Description

Two set ups were built: one for 2D image capture and one for 3D characteristics acquisition.

2D set-up was built to measure only location errors, so illumination and distance camera–subject were maintained unchanged. Two diffuse lights offered controlled illumination conditions. CCD was placed firmly in front of the subject. Subjects were forced to change its pose between acquisitions of two consecutive images.

The 2D database is formed by 29 subjects (22 male and 7 female) with 12 images per subject. 8 images were used for train and 4 for test. Image size is 320 x 240 pixels with face covering great part of the image.

3D set-up was built by a stereo pair of CCD cameras. Figure 1 shows the considered architecture.

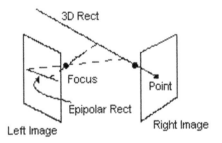
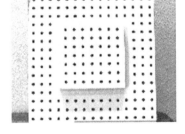

Figure 1. A diagram of the stereo geometry considered.   **Figure 2.** Calibration plate.

Camera calibration is a crucial phase in most vision systems and a first step in 3D reconstruction. Using a plate calibration is possible to obtain a set of 3D data. Figure 2 shows the calibration plate used. It has 193 points distributed over two planes. The 3D database is formed by 20 subjects (10 male and 10 female) with 8 images per subject (than belong to 4 stereo pairs). Four images were used for train and four for test.

3   Algorithm Description

3.1   2D System

Face verification process is split in three parts: Face location, PCA computation and classification.

3.1.1   Face Location

In this step, background is eliminated. Then a convolution with a face template is done. When the convolution reaches the maximum over the images, a window containing the face is extracted. Once the face is located, a set of "correct located faces" is built. These images were considered for computing PCA matrix and training all classifiers. To test location errors, three different test set were built. An initial test set was built in a similar way as explained before, considering the maximum of convolution ("correct located images"). To obtain two test sets, small displacements were applied in both axes (0 and 20 pixels). This gives us two sets of images, each set corresponds to images displaced the same value. Final dimension was 130 x 140 pixels. In this step all images were also converted from colour to grey scale (Figure 3 and 4).

Figure 3 and 4. A correct located face and the same face, but displaced 20 pixels in both axes

3.1.2   PCA Computation

PCA transformation matrix is computed using a number of eigenvectors that retains almost 100% of the initial variance. Only one PCA matrix is computed with the "correct located faces" set. In our experiment eight images per subject are considered to compute PCA matrix. Our tests show that 150 eigenvalues are needed to explain the 99,9% of the variance.

3.2   3D System

The geometrical characteristics are constructed with facial and cranial points similar to those used by forensic doctors and legal police. Initially thirty points were considered, but only the fourteen most robust were selected. These points had to be manually introduced in the images captured by the stereo pair and after that the characteristics in the 3D space were calculated. To minimize the error of the manual location of these points, the epipolar rectification (see Figure 3) was considered.

3.3 Classification

Three classifiers has been considered: K-nearest neighbours (KNN), Artificial Neural Networks: Radial Basis Function (RBF) and Support Vector Machine (SVM).

KNN is a simple and linear classifier but it result can be considered as an initial clue of the spatial configuration of face clusters. K=1 and k=3 has been considered. RBF has been used as an artificial neural network classifier for face verification. In our experiment, Gaussian functions considered are symmetric and centred in the middle of each face subject cluster. SVM could be easily used in verification problems (recognizing one subject against rest). In our experiment, linear kernel has been considered.

4   Experimental Results

4.1   2D Results

Results are represented in a ROC (Receiver Operator Characteristic) curve, one curve per classifier and location condition There are four possible experimental outcomes: true positive, true negative, false positive and false negative.

KNN classifier output is more reliable if distance is low, so a positive verification has been considered when output value is smaller than acceptance threshold. SVM and RBF provide opposite results, so positive verification has been considered when the output value is larger than acceptance threshold. The magnitudes used as threshold for each classifier are KNN Euclidean distance, RBF output neuron value and SVM function decision value. Graphical results are obtained in a cross validation procedure.

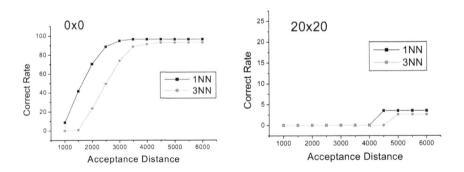

Figure 5. KNN results for each face location

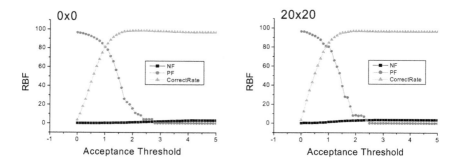

Figure 6. RBF results for each face location

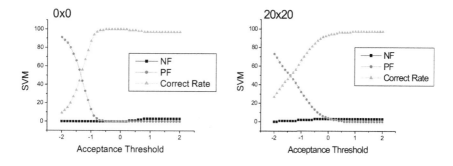

Figure 7. SVM results for each face location

4.2 3D Results

Classification conditions are the same as 2D. Figures 8, 9 and 10 show the results.

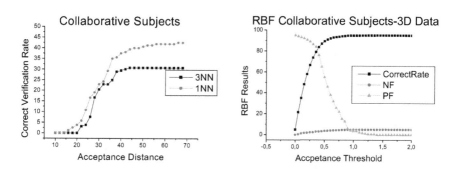

Figure 8. KNN results. 3D Data.   **Figure 9.** RBF results. 3D Data.

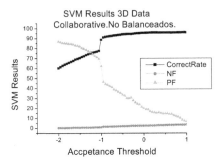

Figure 10. SVM results. 3D Data

5   Conclusions

Given our 2D dataset, worst results have been achieved with KNN. SVM reduces False Positive and False Negative percentages in all the location cases. RBF is more sensitive to location errors (Figures 5, 6 and 7).

Results obtained by the system applied to the 3D data, have been worst due to the important error location introduced in the manual point selection stage. KNN results are really poor, but with a better classifier like SVM, correct rate increases it value significantly (Figures 8, 9 and 10).

References

[1] M. Turk, A. Pentland. Eigenfaces for Recognition. Journal of Cognitive Neuroscience. V 3, N 1, P 71-86. 1991.

[2] P. N. Belhumeur, J. P. Hespanha, D. J. Kriegman. Eigenfaces vs Fisherfaces: Recognition using class specific linear projection. IEEE Transactions in Pattern Analysis and Machine Intelligence, Vol 19. N 7 P 711-720. July 1997.

[3] L. Wiskott, J-M Fellous, N. Krüger, C. von der Malsburg. Face Recognition by Elastic Bunch Graph Matching. IEEE Transactions on Pattern Analysis and Machine Intelligence. Vol 19, Nº 7. p 775-789. Jul. 1997.

[4] P. S. Penev, J. J. Atick. Local feature analysis: a general statistical theory for object representation. Network: Computation in Neural Systems. V 7, N 3, P 477-500, 1996.

[5] J. J. Atick, P. A. Griffin, A. N. Redlich. Statistical approach to shape from shading: reconstruction of 3D face surfaces from single 2D images. Neural Computation. V 8. N 6. P 1321-1340. Aug. 1996.

[6] R. Lengagne, P. Fua, O. Monga. 3D stereo reconstruction of human faces driven by differential constraints. Image and Vision Computing. V 18. N 4. P 337-343. Mar 2000.

[7] R. L. Hsu. Face detection and modelling for recognition. PhD. Thesis. Michigan State University. Dpt. Computer Science and Engineering. 2002.

[8] T. Joachims, *Making large-scale SVM Learning Practical*. Advances in Kernel Methods Support Vector Learning, B. Schölkopf and C. Burges and A. Smola (ed.), MIT-Press, 1999.

Author Index

Akarun, L., 138
Alpaydın, E., 138

Bicego, M., 126
Bigun, J., 1
Boyd, J.E., 19

Cabello, E., 153
Campadelli, P., 147
Castellani, U., 126
Cipolla, R., 114
Conde, C., 153

Fierrez-Aguilar, J., 1
Franceschi, E., 91

Gökberk, B., 138
Gonzales-Rodriguez, J., 1
Grosso, E., 69

Iacono, G., 126
Irfanoglu, M.O., 138

Lagorio, A., 69
Lanzarotti, R., 147
Little, J.J., 19

Maimon, D., 105
Maltoni, D., 43
Mata, S., 153
Murino, V., 126

Odone, F., 91
Ortega-Garcia, J., 1

Sá
Stenger, B., 114

Thayananthan, A., 114
Tistarelli, M., 69
Torr, P.H.S., 114

Verri, A., 91

Yeshurun, Y., 105

Lecture Notes in Computer Science

For information about Vols. 1–3424

please contact your bookseller or Springer

Vol. 3535: M. Steffen, G. Zavattaro (Eds.), Formal Methods for Open Object-Based Distributed Systems. X, 323 pages. 2005.

Vol. 3532: A. Gómez-Pérez, J. Euzenat (Eds.), The Semantic Web: Research and Applications. XV, 728 pages. 2005.

Vol. 3526: S.B. Cooper, B. Löwe, L. Torenvliet (Eds.), New Computational Paradigms. XVII, 574 pages. 2005.

Vol. 3525: A.E. Abdallah, C.B. Jones, J.W. Sanders (Eds.), Communicating Sequential Processes. XIV, 321 pages. 2005.

Vol. 3524: R. Barták, M. Milano (Eds.), Integration of AI and OR Techniques in Constraint Programming for Combinatorial Problems. XI, 320 pages. 2005.

Vol. 3523: J.S. Marques, N.P. de la Blanca, P. Pina (Eds.), Pattern Recognition and Image Analysis, Part II. XXVI, 733 pages. 2005.

Vol. 3522: J.S. Marques, N.P. de la Blanca, P. Pina (Eds.), Pattern Recognition and Image Analysis, Part I. XXVI, 703 pages. 2005.

Vol. 3520: O. Pastor, J. Falcão e Cunha (Eds.), Advanced Information Systems Engineering. XVI, 584 pages. 2005.

Vol. 3518: T.B. Ho, D. Cheung, H. Li (Eds.), Advances in Knowledge Discovery and Data Mining. XXI, 864 pages. 2005. (Subseries LNAI).

Vol. 3517: H.S. Baird, D.P. Lopresti (Eds.), Human Interactive Proofs. IX, 143 pages. 2005.

Vol. 3516: V.S. Sunderam, G.D. van Albada, P.M.A. Sloot, J.J. Dongarra (Eds.), Computational Science – ICCS 2005, Part III. LXIII, 1143 pages. 2005.

Vol. 3515: V.S. Sunderam, G.D. van Albada, P.M.A. Sloot, J.J. Dongarra (Eds.), Computational Science – ICCS 2005, Part II. LXIII, 1101 pages. 2005.

Vol. 3514: V.S. Sunderam, G.D. van Albada, P.M.A. Sloot, J.J. Dongarra (Eds.), Computational Science – ICCS 2005, Part I. LXIII, 1089 pages. 2005.

Vol. 3513: A. Montoyo, R. Mu\˜noz, E. Métais (Eds.), Natural Language Processing and Information Systems. XII, 408 pages. 2005.

Vol. 3510: T. Braun, G. Carle, Y. Koucheryavy, V. Tsaoussidis (Eds.), Wired/Wireless Internet Communications. XIV, 366 pages. 2005.

Vol. 3509: M. Jünger, V. Kaibel (Eds.), Integer Programming and Combinatorial Optimization. XI, 484 pages. 2005.

Vol. 3508: P. Bresciani, P. Giorgini, B. Henderson-Sellers, G. Low, M. Winikoff (Eds.), Agent-Oriented Information Systems II. X, 227 pages. 2005. (Subseries LNAI).

Vol. 3507: F. Crestani, I. Ruthven (Eds.), Information Context: Nature, Impact, and Role. XIII, 253 pages. 2005.

Vol. 3505: V. Gorodetsky, J. Liu, V.A. Skormin (Eds.), Autonomous Intelligent Systems: Agents and Data Mining. XIII, 303 pages. 2005. (Subseries LNAI).

Vol. 3503: S.E. Nikoletseas (Ed.), Experimental and Efficient Algorithms. XV, 624 pages. 2005.

Vol. 3502: F. Khendek, R. Dssouli (Eds.), Testing of Communicating Systems. X, 381 pages. 2005.

Vol. 3501: B. Kégl, G. Lapalme (Eds.), Advances in Artificial Intelligence. XV, 458 pages. 2005. (Subseries LNAI).

Vol. 3500: S. Miyano, J. Mesirov, S. Kasif, S. Istrail, P. Pevzner, M. Waterman (Eds.), Research in Computational Molecular Biology. XVII, 632 pages. 2005. (Subseries LNBI).

Vol. 3499: A. Pelc, M. Raynal (Eds.), Structural Information and Communication Complexity. X, 323 pages. 2005.

Vol. 3498: J. Wang, X. Liao, Z. Yi (Eds.), Advances in Neural Networks – ISNN 2005, Part III. L, 1077 pages. 2005.

Vol. 3497: J. Wang, X. Liao, Z. Yi (Eds.), Advances in Neural Networks – ISNN 2005, Part II. L, 947 pages. 2005.

Vol. 3496: J. Wang, X. Liao, Z. Yi (Eds.), Advances in Neural Networks – ISNN 2005, Part II. L, 1055 pages. 2005.

Vol. 3495: P. Kantor, G. Muresan, F. Roberts, D.D. Zeng, F.-Y. Wang, H. Chen, R.C. Merkle (Eds.), Intelligence and Security Informatics. XVIII, 674 pages. 2005.

Vol. 3494: R. Cramer (Ed.), Advances in Cryptology – EUROCRYPT 2005. XIV, 576 pages. 2005.

Vol. 3493: N. Fuhr, M. Lalmas, S. Malik, Z. Szlávik (Eds.), Advances in XML Information Retrieval. XI, 438 pages. 2005.

Vol. 3492: P. Blache, E. Stabler, J. Busquets, R. Moot (Eds.), Logical Aspects of Computational Linguistics. X, 363 pages. 2005. (Subseries LNAI).

Vol. 3489: G.T. Heineman, I. Crnkovic, H.W. Schmidt, J.A. Stafford, C. Szyperski, K. Wallnau (Eds.), Component-Based Software Engineering. XI, 358 pages. 2005.

Vol. 3488: M.-S. Hacid, N.V. Murray, Z.W. Raś, S. Tsumoto (Eds.), Foundations of Intelligent Systems. XIII, 700 pages. 2005. (Subseries LNAI).

Vol. 3486: T. Helleseth, D. Sarwate, H.-Y. Song, K. Yang (Eds.), Sequences and Their Applications - SETA 2004. XII, 451 pages. 2005.

Vol. 3483: O. Gervasi, M.L. Gavrilova, V. Kumar, A. Laganà, H.P. Lee, Y. Mun, D. Taniar, C.J.K. Tan (Eds.), Computational Science and Its Applications – ICCSA 2005, Part IV. XXVII, 1362 pages. 2005.

Vol. 3482: O. Gervasi, M.L. Gavrilova, V. Kumar, A. Laganà, H.P. Lee, Y. Mun, D. Taniar, C.J.K. Tan (Eds.), Computational Science and Its Applications – ICCSA 2005, Part III. LXVI, 1340 pages. 2005.

Vol. 3481: O. Gervasi, M.L. Gavrilova, V. Kumar, A. Laganà, H.P. Lee, Y. Mun, D. Taniar, C.J.K. Tan (Eds.), Computational Science and Its Applications – ICCSA 2005, Part II. LXIV, 1316 pages. 2005.

Vol. 3480: O. Gervasi, M.L. Gavrilova, V. Kumar, A. Laganà, H.P. Lee, Y. Mun, D. Taniar, C.J.K. Tan (Eds.), Computational Science and Its Applications – ICCSA 2005, Part I. LXV, 1234 pages. 2005.

Vol. 3479: T. Strang, C. Linnhoff-Popien (Eds.), Location- and Context-Awareness. XII, 378 pages. 2005.

Vol. 3478: C. Jermann, A. Neumaier, D. Sam (Eds.), Global Optimization and Constraint Satisfaction. XIII, 193 pages. 2005.

Vol. 3477: P. Herrmann, V. Issarny, S. Shiu (Eds.), Trust Management. XII, 426 pages. 2005.

Vol. 3475: N. Guelfi (Ed.), Rapid Integration of Software Engineering Techniques. X, 145 pages. 2005.

Vol. 3468: H.W. Gellersen, R. Want, A. Schmidt (Eds.), Pervasive Computing. XIII, 347 pages. 2005.

Vol. 3467: J. Giesl (Ed.), Term Rewriting and Applications. XIII, 517 pages. 2005.

Vol. 3465: M. Bernardo, A. Bogliolo (Eds.), Formal Methods for Mobile Computing. VII, 271 pages. 2005.

Vol. 3464: S.A. Brueckner, G.D.M. Serugendo, A. Karageorgos, R. Nagpal (Eds.), Engineering Self-Organising Systems. XIII, 299 pages. 2005. (Subseries LNAI).

Vol. 3463: M. Dal Cin, M. Kaâniche, A. Pataricza (Eds.), Dependable Computing - EDCC 2005. XVI, 472 pages. 2005.

Vol. 3462: R. Boutaba, K.C. Almeroth, R. Puigjaner, S. Shen, J.P. Black (Eds.), NETWORKING 2005. XXX, 1483 pages. 2005.

Vol. 3461: P. Urzyczyn (Ed.), Typed Lambda Calculi and Applications. XI, 433 pages. 2005.

Vol. 3460: Ö. Babaoglu, M. Jelasity, A. Montresor, C. Fetzer, S. Leonardi, A. van Moorsel, M. van Steen (Eds.), Self-star Properties in Complex Information Systems. IX, 447 pages. 2005.

Vol. 3459: R. Kimmel, N.A. Sochen, J. Weickert (Eds.), Scale Space and PDE Methods in Computer Vision. XI, 634 pages. 2005.

Vol. 3458: P. Herrero, M.S. Pérez, V. Robles (Eds.), Scientific Applications of Grid Computing. X, 208 pages. 2005.

Vol. 3456: H. Rust, Operational Semantics for Timed Systems. XII, 223 pages. 2005.

Vol. 3455: H. Treharne, S. King, M. Henson, S. Schneider (Eds.), ZB 2005: Formal Specification and Development in Z and B. XV, 493 pages. 2005.

Vol. 3454: J.-M. Jacquet, G.P. Picco (Eds.), Coordination Models and Languages. X, 299 pages. 2005.

Vol. 3453: L. Zhou, B.C. Ooi, X. Meng (Eds.), Database Systems for Advanced Applications. XXVII, 929 pages. 2005.

Vol. 3452: F. Baader, A. Voronkov (Eds.), Logic for Programming, Artificial Intelligence, and Reasoning. XI, 562 pages. 2005. (Subseries LNAI).

Vol. 3450: D. Hutter, M. Ullmann (Eds.), Security in Pervasive Computing. XI, 239 pages. 2005.

Vol. 3449: F. Rothlauf, J. Branke, S. Cagnoni, D.W. Corne, R. Drechsler, Y. Jin, P. Machado, E. Marchiori, J. Romero, G.D. Smith, G. Squillero (Eds.), Applications of Evolutionary Computing. XX, 631 pages. 2005.

Vol. 3448: G.R. Raidl, J. Gottlieb (Eds.), Evolutionary Computation in Combinatorial Optimization. XI, 271 pages. 2005.

Vol. 3447: M. Keijzer, A. Tettamanzi, P. Collet, J.v. Hemert, M. Tomassini (Eds.), Genetic Programming. XIII, 382 pages. 2005.

Vol. 3444: M. Sagiv (Ed.), Programming Languages and Systems. XIII, 439 pages. 2005.

Vol. 3443: R. Bodik (Ed.), Compiler Construction. XI, 305 pages. 2005.

Vol. 3442: M. Cerioli (Ed.), Fundamental Approaches to Software Engineering. XIII, 373 pages. 2005.

Vol. 3441: V. Sassone (Ed.), Foundations of Software Science and Computational Structures. XVIII, 521 pages. 2005.

Vol. 3440: N. Halbwachs, L.D. Zuck (Eds.), Tools and Algorithms for the Construction and Analysis of Systems. XVII, 588 pages. 2005.

Vol. 3439: R.H. Deng, F. Bao, H. Pang, J. Zhou (Eds.), Information Security Practice and Experience. XII, 424 pages. 2005.

Vol. 3438: H. Christiansen, P.R. Skadhauge, J. Villadsen (Eds.), Constraint Solving and Language Processing. VIII, 205 pages. 2005. (Subseries LNAI).

Vol. 3437: T. Gschwind, C. Mascolo (Eds.), Software Engineering and Middleware. X, 245 pages. 2005.

Vol. 3436: B. Bouyssounouse, J. Sifakis (Eds.), Embedded Systems Design. XV, 492 pages. 2005.

Vol. 3434: L. Brun, M. Vento (Eds.), Graph-Based Representations in Pattern Recognition. XII, 384 pages. 2005.

Vol. 3433: S. Bhalla (Ed.), Databases in Networked Information Systems. VII, 319 pages. 2005.

Vol. 3432: M. Beigl, P. Lukowicz (Eds.), Systems Aspects in Organic and Pervasive Computing - ARCS 2005. X, 265 pages. 2005.

Vol. 3431: C. Dovrolis (Ed.), Passive and Active Network Measurement. XII, 374 pages. 2005.

Vol. 3430: S. Tsumoto, T. Yamaguchi, M. Numao, H. Motoda (Eds.), Active Mining. XII, 349 pages. 2005. (Subseries LNAI).

Vol. 3429: E. Andres, G. Damiand, P. Lienhardt (Eds.), Discrete Geometry for Computer Imagery. X, 428 pages. 2005.

Vol. 3428: Y.-J. Kwon, A. Bouju, C. Claramunt (Eds.), Web and Wireless Geographical Information Systems. XII, 255 pages. 2005.

Vol. 3427: G. Kotsis, O. Spaniol (Eds.), Wireless Systems and Mobility in Next Generation Internet. VIII, 249 pages. 2005.